HOW TO PLAY GOLF

BY

HARRY VARDON

WITH FORTY-EIGHT ILLUSTRATIONS

SIXTEENTH EDITION

METHUEN & CO. LTD.
36 ESSEX STREET W.C.
LONDON

First Published . . . . September 26th 1912
Second, Third, and Fourth Editions . . October   1912
Fifth Edition . . . . March   1913
Sixth Edition . . . . September   1913
Seventh Edition . . . . October   1913
Eighth Edition . . . . April   1914
Ninth Edition . . . . September   1914
Tenth Edition . . . . March   1917
Eleventh Edition . . . . February   1919
Twelfth Edition . . . . September   1919
Thirteenth Edition . . . . May   1920
Fourteenth Edition . . . . March   1921
Fifteenth Edition . . . . September   1921
Sixteenth Edition   1922

Harry Vardon

PREFACE

AMONGST games, golf has a nature peculiarly its own, and in no respect is its distinctiveness more marked than in the circumstance that it allows its devotees practically a free hand in the choice of the implements, the ball, and the extent and general characteristics of the playing ground. Golf, then, is apt to alter considerably as the seasons come and go. It is a game in which the sentiment of liberty holds sway. In point of fact, it has changed a great deal during recent years, and for that reason I offer no apology for appearing a second time as the author of a book of instruction on a subject which I have made my life-study. My first was "The Complete Golfer," which is still popular. The present work does not replace that, but supplements it in the light of recent developments.

Golf demands deep thought till the end of one's playing days, and, as one grows older, ideas continue to present themselves in connexion with the principles of executing shots. If I may say with frankness what I think, I will express the opinion that many amateurs fail to attain that degree of success which is within their reach for the simple reason that they do not reflect sufficiently upon the possibilities, especially where small points are concerned. The professional has to think, because golf is his livelihood; that, in the abstract, is why he excels. He gives close attention to details, and knows the cause of every effect.

In this volume, I have tried to explain to the full the twin subjects of cause and effect on the links. If the golfer of ability finds some hints which he learnt in the long ago, let him recollect the needs of the moderate performer. And, in any case, even the short-handicap player may not be the worse for a refreshment of his memory in matters of the fundamental rules of action. It is in the more advanced kind of golf that the chief changes in methods (the natural corollary of changes in materials) have taken place. I have thought over them with care, and set down what I regard as the most profitable means of playing the game to-day; the methods which I personally employ.

In this connexion, let me describe an experience which often falls to the professional who is called upon to travel considerably in pursuit of golf. A little while ago I visited a course which I had not seen for seven or eight years. To mention one particular hole will be sufficient for my purpose. It had not been altered since the time of my introduction to it. Moreover, I had to play it on the second occasion in practically the same circumstances, in the matter of weather, as seven or eight years ago—that is to say, in a strong right-to-left wind. In the first instance, I decided to hit my drive into the wind and impart pull to the ball so as to gain distance by the effect of the spin and the wind coming into kindly co-operation on my behalf when the shot was nearing its end. On the later occasion I found myself playing what I regard as the up-to-date game. I hit an almost straight drive with a suspicion of cut on it so as to bring the ball into the wind at the finish of its flight. Each constituted I think, the right tactics at the time of their employment. But why did I alter? Because the ball had changed. Now that the ball is so resilient and so susceptible to the slightest movement which accentuates the run, the intentional pull is the most dangerous shot in the game. To keep it under perfect control when the ground is hard and the course is narrow is so difficult as to involve a very big risk. Here, then, is a concrete example of the way in which golf has changed.

In regard to the photographs which accompany these pages, I should like to say that they were taken in the actual process of accomplishing shots that produced precisely the desired effects. I can assure the reader that they represent the player in the positions which he knows, after many years of study, to be correct—or, in the case of the illustrations of wrong swings, incorrect. In the background of the pictures will be noticed a high pole. I had it put there so as to throw into relief the position of the head and body during the different stages of the swings. The device in front of several of the illustrations also makes clear the absence of movement, or the unhappy movement of the head. The different stances are well defined by the position of the feet in the chalk-line figure in which the photographs were taken. I have not included the rules of golf. For one thing, they are changed from time to time, and for another, they are very easily accessible to anybody who wants them.

I greatly desire to thank Mr Robert E. Howard for the part which he has played in the production of this volume. Let me explain how it has been born. I love teaching golf; I like the task far better than that of competing in championships. I can write down just how I make every shot and why I make it that way, but to put it into the form of book instruction is a different matter. Mr Howard has taken in hand my notes, arranged them in order and rounded off the rough edges. For the purpose of " How to Play Golf," I have exhausted myself, I think, of all the knowledge of the subject I ever possessed, and I trust that the result may be helpful to the many thousands of people who wish to wake up one fine day to find themselves at scratch, or better, on the links.

H. V.

CONTENTS

CHAP.   PAGE

I. THE TREND OF THE GAME . . . 13

II. GOLF COURSE ARCHITECTURE . . . 25

III. EQUIPMENT: SOME TRIFLES THAT AMOUNT TO
     MUCH 39

IV. TWO ESSENTIALS OF SUCCESS . . . 52

V. HOW TO DRIVE 64

VI. CLEEK AND IRON SHOTS . . . 78

VII. MASHIE SHOTS 87

VIII. ON THE GREEN 100

IX. RECOVERING FROM DIFFICULTIES . . 110

X. THE "PUSH" SHOT 121

XI. GOLF IN A WIND 130

XII. SOME COMMON FAULTS 143

XIII. PROMINENT PLAYERS AND THEIR METHODS . 156

XIV. SUMMER GOLF AND WINTER GOLF . . 166

XV. THE GAME ABROAD 171

INDEX 181

9

LIST OF ILLUSTRATIONS

HARRY VARDON . . . . . *Frontispiece*

FACING PAGE

A GOOD TEST FOR THE TEE SHOT IN MODERN GOLF   28

GRIPS RIGHT AND WRONG 60

THE OVERLAPPING GRIP 62

THE DRIVE OR BRASSIE SHOT 72

COMING DOWN 74

FAULTY MOVEMENTS 76

THE CLEEK SHOT 82

THE IRON SHOT 84

THE ORDINARY MASHIE SHOT 90

FINISH OF THE ORDINARY MASHIE SHOT . . . 92

THE MASHIE SHOT WITH CUT 94

THE MASHIE SHOT WITH CUT 96

THE RUNNING-UP SHOT 98

THE RUNNING-UP SHOT 99

PUTTING 104

BUNKERED 112

BUNKERED 114

                                                    FACING PAGE
THE " PUSH " CLEEK SHOT   126

THE " PUSH " CLEEK SHOT   128

A DISTINCTION WITH A DIFFERENCE   .   .   .   129

INTENTIONAL SLICING AND PULLING   138

IN THE WIND   142

IN THE BEGINNING   150

IN THE BEGINNING   151

The illustrations are from action photographs specially taken by Arthur Ullyett.

HOW TO PLAY GOLF

CHAPTER I

THE TREND OF THE GAME

FOR the modern beginner at golf to attain a fair degree of proficiency is, if he pursue his object in the proper way, an immeasurably easier matter than it was for any of us who started to play in the days of the gutta-percha ball. And it is possible to exhibit a deal of Christian philosophy in congratulating the newer inhabitants of the golfing world in respect to this facility, because I am certain that those people who went through the mill in the earlier days of the pastime obtained, of sheer necessity, a knowledge of shots such as the rubber-cored ball, under present conditions, never encourages. That knowledge has been the great and faithful stand-by of the older players in times of strenuous competition with younger rivals.

On a recent summer's afternoon, when the ball had been soaring and bounding from well-hit tee shots over some 300 yards of country, when the course, even as we finished at five o'clock, seemed to be alive at every point with folk in full enjoyment of this wonderful game, I fell to thinking in a more or less haphazard way of the developments

which had taken place in golf during the time
that I had known it.   And I could not help mar-
velling; I could not help rejoicing at having been
lucky enough to live through what had been surely
the most crowded age that ever pastime knew.

It is just about twenty years since I began
to make a deep and earnest study of golf.   Of
course, I have played it a good deal longer than
that, but my earlier efforts were of a rather light-
hearted description, and I had no idea that the
game would ever be more to me than a means
of occasional diversion.   Twenty years represent,
perhaps, a considerable portion of a person's
life, but they pass quickly when events move so
rapidly as they have moved in golf.   Matters of
the moment and possibilities of the immediate
future are apt to completely fill the mind; and when
one sits down to reflect on the transformation
that two decades have produced, memories and
the comparisons which they engender appear to
one almost in the nature of revelations.

There has been no period in the history of the
game so pregnant with evolution as the past
seven or eight years, since golfers began to understand the possibilities of the rubber-cored ball
and to adapt themselves to the new manner of
playing provoked by that revolutionary invention.
For, so far as one can discuss such a matter in
a general way, a method of hitting the shots different from that which prevailed in the days of the
gutta-percha ball has most certainly come into
vogue.   Such, at least, is the opinion which I
have formed after travelling many thousands of
miles in pursuit of golf, visiting many hundreds
of courses, and seeing the pastime during these
twenty years in all its phases; and I will endeavour
to justify the belief before I reach the end of
this chapter.

That the rubber-cored ball has done, and is still doing, a great deal to spoil golf as an athletic and scientific recreation I feel convinced. It is still a great game, and nothing can kill the peculiar fascination which it exercises over its devotees, and yet it seems to me to be a different sort of game from that which we played with the gutta-percha ball. But here I may perhaps be permitted to say that, regretful as I am at the reign of the rubber-core, which has removed much of the old necessity for thought and grace of style, I fear that nothing but indescribable chaos would result if the suggestion to standardize the gutty for competitions, put forward in several influential quarters, were adopted. We must not forget that, for countless thousands of people, the rubber-core has greatly increased the enjoyment of golf by making the game much more easy. It may be that they can only spare the time to play two days a week, and they want to extract the maximum amount of pleasure that those two days and the opposition will allow. Nothing would induce them to return to the gutty (or, as it would be in many cases, play with it for the first time), and personally I do not blame them. Then what would be the position? It would be a state of confusion far worse than anything which now exists, although the present situation truly offers food for thought. The leading players (indeed all golfers who like to take part in competitions) would have to keep in practice with the gutty. They could not be expected to use that ball one day and a rubber-core the next. At least, if they tried to do so, the perplexity arising from the frequent change would bring despair to their souls.

The competition golfer who practised with the gutty would scarcely dare to so much as look at a man playing with a rubber-core. I have a vivid recollection of an episode bearing on that point. In the open championship at Hoylake, in 1902, when a few rubber-cores were employed, I was coupled with Peter M'Ewen, who was one of the converts to the innovation. Like the majority, I remained faithful to the gutty. I happened to be driving rather well, and was generally a little way in front of M'Ewen from the tee, so that he usually had to play "the odd" in the approaches.

After seeing him pitch his Haskell short of the green for the ball to perform the remainder of the journey along the ground, I was absolutely nonplussed. I simply could not get up with a mashie. Repeatedly I told myself that I must not take any notice of what his ball had done; that I must think only of what my ball would do. But, as every golfer knows, the inclination to judge the run by that which the other player obtains is irresistible. I tried to pitch farther and farther to allow for the difference between the rubber-core and the gutty, but something (I suppose the knowledge of how much too far he would be if he hit as I intended to hit) seemed to hold me back, and I was always short. I lost that championship by a stroke. I have no regrets, because my old friend, "Sandy" Herd, deserved a championship if ever man merited that honour. I have mentioned the matter solely to show what distraction might be visited upon the user of the gutty if he merely went out and saw other people playing with rubber-cores. And there would be so many of the latter that he would find them hard to dodge.

The confusion in the matter of arranging matches would be indescribable. As an instance, let me relate a little experience. At one time I played many games with an amateur who had the shortest swing I ever saw. He was a fine sportsman, and as pleasant an opponent as I have met, but I cannot truthfully say that I admired his style. It was like the action of a man cracking a whip "underhand," so to speak. He simply took the club back a little way, and gave the ball a sharp tap. He hardly ever missed a shot, but, of course, with the gutty he could not get sufficient distance. I could give him a stroke a hole and a beating. When the Haskells came over from America, he was among the few who obtained early supplies at huge prices. Those were the times when a Haskell was cheap at a sovereign. He brought a sample out to play me one day, and I soon discovered that, using a gutty, I could hardly give him a third. He played me many more games with this difference in the ball still prevailing, and he, with a third, beat me as often as I beat him. He subsequently distinguished himself in open scratch competitions, and was finalist in a county championship. This may be an exceptional case (the rubber-core suited the style of my erstwhile opponent even better than that of the average player), but it affords an indication of the chaos that would prevail if we had some players employing the rubber ball and others suffering in the cause of difficult golf with the gutta-percha article.

No, deeply as I grieve at the passing of the gutty, I do not see how it is to be reinstated, even to the limited extent of its being made a standard ball for championships. The rubber-core is established, and nothing can shift it without creating fresh embarrassment. It has had one useful effect. I believe that it has been responsible to some extent for the enormously increased popularity of golf. By making the game easier, it has flattered many people into the belief that they are

better players than is the case, and that they can
master the finer points of the pastime in a period
which, in due course, they discover to be hopelessly insufficient for the purpose. That may be
good or bad, according to the point of view. In
the sense that it affords greater enjoyment for the
majority, it is good. In the sense that it does
away with the old incentive to deep thought and
consummate skill, it is bad. Golf will never be an
easy game, nor will it ever again be quite the
game that it was before the rubber-core ball made
its appearance.

Personally, I am convinced that while the scores
are getting lower, as they must do with a ball
that affords such help, the standard of golf in
general is deteriorating. I have put down the
remark not merely as a result of a sudden
inspiration. I have held the opinion for several
years, and expressed it to friends. Nothing
has happened to justify an alteration in my
belief. Wherever I have gone, the same evidence
of a falling-off in the intrinsic quality of the golf
has been manifest, and it is attributable to the
influence of the rubber-cored ball. For one thing,
players have become careless. The miss is sometimes better than the hit; and everybody is aware
of the fact. There was wisdom in the remark of
one of my opponents who had topped his mashie
stroke to within holing distance: "Any old shot
will do nowadays." All too often it will do remarkably well. In the time of the gutty, a
player knew that if he perpetrated a bad stroke,
he would be punished. He would be short, or,
if his ball reached a bunker, it would not jump the
hazard. The knowledge that there was no mercy
for those who erred impelled him to be careful.

There was only one way to play every shot;
it had to be played properly. With the present

ball there are several ways of obtaining the desired end, and, what is worse, a good stroke is
not infrequently ruined by the resilient ball light-
ing on very keen ground and bounding away into
all sorts of trouble.

I can recall plenty of instances where, in suc-
ceeding rounds, I have played at a certain hole
shots that seemed to be identical. But while one
has been a success, the other has been a failure.
There was a case in point in the German open
championship at Baden-Baden in 1911. I won the
competition all right, and I am not complaining
about the incident, which was of the kind from
which we all suffer in turn. I offer it as one
among many proofs that might be given of the
freakishness of modern golf. At a short hole
I pitched to what was evidently the right spot;
for the ball ran up close to the pin, and I got
a 2. In the next round, I made what appeared
to be an equally good shot, but the ball struck
such ground that it stopped short of the plateau
green. For no apparent reason it went over the
green from the second shot, and I escaped with
a 6! Nemesis may not always be so brutal as
that when you misjudge a carry by a yard, but
it often happens that a stroke is either gained
or lost through no extra clever or extra bad play.

I have declared that the game is deteriorating,
and I have made the statement with such assurance
because I feel that I can tell by my own golf.
I was fortunate enough in 1911 to gain the open
championship and a nice lot of other contests,
but I am absolutely certain that the actual quality
of my golf was four strokes a round worse
than it was with the gutta-percha ball. I
say this in all sincerity, after considering
fully just what is meant by a difference of
four strokes in eighteen holes. The scores,

of course, were lower (in the ordinary way you
can hardly help doing a round with the rubber-
core that is low by comparison with a gutty ball
return), but as regards the real value of the play,
my own has deteriorated to the extent indicated.
That being so, the falling-off must have been
general, or I surely should not have won anything. Perhaps I happened to have nothing but
good fortune, although I cannot remember en-
joying more than a fair share of it.

Whenever in the old days I took an iron club
in my hand, I could tell to within two or three
yards not only where the ball would pitch, but
where it would stop. That was possible for any
player who practised assiduously with the gutty.
It is certainly not possible with the rubber-core.
In fact, I fancy everybody is, at times, between
two minds as to how it would be best to play
a really ordinary shot. No game would be
worth pursuing unless luck entered into it in
some measure, but the rubber-core in golf has
introduced the elements of indecision and uncertainty into the player's mind. In that respect
golf has become more of "a thinking game"
than ever; the misfortune is that the thoughts
seldom lead to clearly-established principles.

There is, however, at least one exception to
this rule. Among the players who have been
trained mainly on the rubber-core, there certainly
seems to be an established and generally practised
mode of executing long shots, and it is a mode
which is affecting the standard of the game.
Reference has been made above to a method of
hitting the shots different from that which prevailed in the gutty days. The difference is that
most people now play for a pull. In the matter
of golf, we are becoming a nation of natural
pullers. This even applies in the majority of

cases to the men who made themselves as near perfect as could be with the gutty ball. I fancy that nearly everybody is standing just a trifle more forward than in former times, in order to produce in some degree the effect of the pull and consequent run. Very rarely do you see a man trying chiefly for the "carry," which is, I venture to assert, the proper and, in the end, most satisfactory way of playing golf.

Naturally, it took some time for golfers to learn the possibilities of the rubber-core. Gradually, however, they realized that the greatest length could be obtained from it by playing a flat shot with pull, with the result that, during recent years, this style of stroke has become predominant. Players of all degrees of ability have discovered it, and they employ it habitually. Many have lighted upon it and made it their manner without setting out in any way to learn deliberately how to pull. It is hard to convince oneself that it looks well, or even that in the end it is profitable. Sometimes the ball flies so low and comes to the ground so soon that one might almost imagine that the player had missed the shot. But no, it is his method, and the ball runs and runs and does all that is necessary.

So far, so good; but where this low-pulled shot is a real menace to the standard of the game is in the fact that it is becoming ingrained in the golfing constitution. It is becoming so essentially a habit that the golfer cannot get out of the way of doing it when it would be to his advantage to know nothing about it. It enters into his iron shots. They, too, are played with pull, because that is his natural way of playing. So that when he finds himself in a situation which demands the old-fashioned kind of pitch shot (and he is often so placed), he is at a disadvantage.

Sooner or later championships, scratch medals, and everything else will be won by players who had not the benefit of learning the game with the gutty. Unless a great change takes place in the present trend of golfing style, all those winners will be pullers by instinct, capable of getting a very fine distance with the long shots, but unable to forget, when executing iron approaches, their natural inclination. Such, at least, is the impression which I have formed after studying the game as deeply as ever since the introduction of the rubber-core, and I cannot think that this phase of the evolution is good.

There is one way in which it can be discouraged. It is by demanding a long carry from every tee. For the short driver (if such a person there be) there could be a way round so that he should not be in trouble every time he reached the limit of his powers. Golf is for the multitude; not for plus and scratch players only; and I realize to the full that it is necessary for the average course to be of a character which will afford enjoyment to moderate players as well as to good ones. But if scope were given for a really big carry from every tee, with a path offered to the shorter driver whereby he would not be punished if he hit the ball properly, albeit he might lose half a shot to the man who accomplished the carry, in these circumstances inherent pulling would be checked. The swing which, in a general way, is undoubtedly getting shorter, would resume its old length and rhythm because the good player, at any rate, would be induced to go for the carry. And that would mean hitting the shot just as it was hit with the gutty. I am aware that this plan would not be practicable in all places, but it would be possible in many.

An instance may perhaps be given of the way

in which the golfer of the rubber-core age is
handicapped. Some time ago I played nine
rounds of a course with a man who, during recent
years, has greatly distinguished himself. He is
a fine golfer, but his style is essentially of the
kind that has become general since the introduction of the rubber-core. One of the holes called
for a carry of quite 190 yards—an exceptionally
fine hole I thought. Perhaps in the same circumstances, anybody else would have thought the
same. A river and a large bunker were among
the obstacles that rendered necessary the big
carry, while on either side were chestnut trees.
It was not surpremely difficult to the gutty-trained
player, and I managed to get on to the green
eight times in nine attempts. My opponent, playing what I would call the golf of the rubber-core
age, did not get on once. He could not carry
far enough. I am mentioning this in no spirit
of arrogance. It simply shows the difficulty
which besets the golfer of modern methods when
the necessity arises for him to abandon the low-
flying shot with pull. He finds that he cannot
easily shake off his habitual mode of operation.
And that necessity will always arise, because if
all the courses in the world could be altered to
suit the peculiarities of the rubber-cored ball,
golfers, being human, would still miss strokes or
send them off the line in such a way as to revive
the need for high shots with little run.

This, then, is why I think it would be best from
every point of view if golfers played for the carry
instead of for the run, and why I suggest that
a long carry from the tee should be encouraged.
For ordinary purposes, that is to say, for the
clubs with a considerable majority of members
who play only about twice a week, and who want
to crowd enjoyment rather than painful experience

into those two days, there is no reason why golf should be made excessively difficult, but there is a difference between very trying holes and those which merely call forth the subterfuge of the pull-and-run stroke. The rubber-core, as compared with the gutty, has not greatly increased the carry; the revolution has been created by the run. Under normal conditions, the Haskell put about twenty yards on to our shots, and I suppose that the latest types of rubber-cores have added about forty yards to the length obtainable with the Haskell. That is, of course, without the aid of wind or sloping ground. The carry in ordinary circumstances has not altered very much, and in continuing the demand for it lies the best chance of preserving some of the qualities of gutty-ball golf which, in the opinion of nearly all who are qualified to judge, was the best kind of golf.

Nowadays, by playing for the pulled shot, it is possible to get truly extraordinary distance. One often reads of record drives, but I am sure that dozens of the longest drives have never been measured. In the summer of 1911, when the ground was so favourable to the run, there must have been lots of shots of more than 400 yards. I know that at the long hole at Totteridge, which measures 540 yards, I was regularly getting on to the green with a drive and a niblick. A mashie for my second would have meant going too far. Players in other places were assuredly having similar experiences. It is all very good fun while it lasts, but it is not good practice for the pastime in its entirety.

CHAPTER II

GOLF COURSE ARCHITECTURE

IT is certain that, if you are going to play golf,
you must have a course on which to play it,
and before proceeding to consider any other
phases of the game, we may reasonably devote
some attention to this essential.

On the manner in which the holes are designed
depends not only the pleasure of the golfer. The
style of architecture influences very considerably
the methods of the habitual user of the course,
and either limits or expands his chances of improvement. Much, naturally, must be governed
by local conditions, but there are certain features
that can be introduced almost anywhere, and the
introduction of which must, I am sure, make for
the common good in tending to combine efficiency
with enjoyment. I have mentioned in the foregoing chapter that I would offer to the golfer
the incentive to try to effect a good carry from
every tee. The reasons are, I hope, satisfactory.
There is not a lot of credit attaching to the
performance of making the ball run along the
ground from the drives. It ought to cover most
of the distance in the air. Since the arrival of the
rubber-cored ball, the outstanding tendency has
been to abandon cross-hazards and substitute

bunkers and various other agents of retribution on the wings, with an occasional pot bunker towards the middle of the course. The consequence is that it pays very well to play the flat running shot; often it does not matter if you top the ball, so long as you keep straight. The top is sometimes more profitable than the cleanly-struck shot which goes slightly off the line.

I feel convinced that the way to restore the old standard of golf, the way to counteract some of the harm done by the rubber-core, is to induce golfers to realize that, in long shots, the ball ought to do most of its work by carry and not by scuttling along the ground. Everybody will be better off in the end for such an appreciation of the true element of the game, because everybody will know better from sheer necessity of practice how to get a ball into the air when executing iron shots. In short, I am appealing for a return to something—but not exactly—like the mode of hazard that prevailed when the gutty ball was in vogue. It has been called many hard names in its time. Truth to tell, the old type of inland bunker, which stretched across the course at right-angles to the fairway, was a very dull, unnatural-looking feature of the green. But it had its good points, which were capable of improvement, and the wave of feeling against it that swept over the land was matter for regret.

I may be assailed with the remark that, if we reinstate the cross-hazard, we shall at once revive the objections to it, chief of which was the fact that it had a sliding scale of difficulty, governed by the strength of the wind. Down wind, it was an easy carry; in the teeth of the gale, it was almost impossible. It may also have occurred to the reader that the carry, to be of any value at all as a restorer of the former kind of shot and to test the good player, would need to be a really long carry, whereupon the poorer players would be reduced to a state of misery. Their best shots would merely end in bunkers.

I have thought of these matters, and I cannot see that they offer insuperable difficulties. The plan here suggested could be put into practice in many places, if not everywhere. It is, in brief, to have the bunker running diagonally across the course, that part of the hazard which is farthest from the player when he stands on the teeing-ground being the direct line to the green. Or a chain of three or four fairly large, deep pot bunkers of different shapes stretching diagonally across the fairway is equally suitable. The point of this scheme is obvious. The player decides for himself first whether he will try to effect the carry at all, and next which line he will take. Under normal conditions, a first-class golfer would go for the farthest point, which, if he played the shot properly, would take him straight towards the hole. At the same time, he would open up the green for his second shot. Under this system of bunkering, the green should be long and narrow, so that a person who had taken other than the direct line for his drive would find an increase in the difficulties of the next stroke. The green would be at an awkward angle for him; the entrance to it would be slanting away from him. It would be spread out invitingly to the player who had made the perfect drive. Consequently, it would pay the inferior golfer to think carefully about his plan of action. He might not care to risk the long carry. He might prefer to pick out part of the hazard nearer to him as a safer carry for the drive. Or he might decide to play short of the far end of the hazard and trust to his second to take him over it, thus keeping the

green well open. In any case, the person who
could hit the longer and better tee shot would
generally gain half a stroke—just about a fitting
reward, I venture to think, for such superiority.
This scheme is, in effect, the scheme which exists
at Prince's Sandwich, which is the finest test of
golf that I have ever sampled. Everybody is
entitled to his opinion, but, personally, I never
hope to play on a better course than Prince's Sandwich. And yet it is by no means a links suited
only to plus and scratch men. On the contrary,
it is immensely popular amongst the great army
of handicap players who have tried it. The
reason is, that no shots on it are impossible to the
player who has mastered the rudiments of the
game. The better golfer attempts the long
carries; the worse golfer contents himself with
the shorter ones. Everybody has the scope for
employing all the proficiency that he possesses,
and the crack does not always come so very well
out of the ordeal since he is often tempted to try
herculean feats, which are almost beyond his
powers. But that, after all, is his own fault.
The poorer player is subjected to equal entice-
ment. It is a fine battle of wits as well as of
power, and, under the conditions brought about
by the rubber-cored ball, it is the best golf that I
know.

The accompanying diagram will afford at a
glance an idea of the principle which I have in
mind. The advantage of this system of architecture is that, except in a most extraordinary gale,
some part of the hazard can always be carried,
and the man who can carry the farther obtains his
due reward. There is need for thought and skill
and power and, indeed, all the qualities that made
golf so great a game in the time of the gutta-
percha ball, and which have been threatened

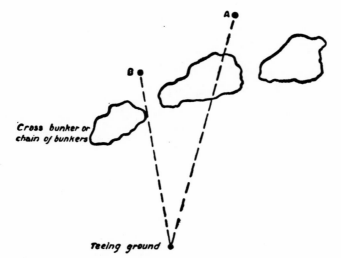

Hole

A

B

Cross bunker or
chain of bunkers

Teeing ground

A good test for the tee shot in modern golf. The player has a choice as to
the length of carry which he will attempt. If he takes the straight line to the
hole, and accomplishes the carry to A, he leaves himself with a comparatively
easy second shot. If he cannot manage the long carry, and prefers to drive to
the spot marked B, he has to approach the hole with a long shot from a difficult
angle. The green should be guarded well on both sides, with the entrance made
easy only for the player who has taken the straight line.

with extinction by the advent of the rubber-core.

In modern golf, no holes are harder to play than the short ones, provided that they are properly designed. I used to think—and say—that three short holes were sufficient on any course, but the character of the game has changed so vastly, and driving has been made so simple by comparison with the difficulties which it presented ten years ago, that I feel that on present-day links even five short holes are not too many. Whatever facilities the ball may afford at the long holes, it is certain that it cannot help anybody at the short ones, and so the latter tend to restore some of the demand for skill. They must, however, call for perfect tee shots. There must be no mercy for the errant player. With care and practice, anybody ought to be able to play a short hole properly. An easy one is the dullest thing known to golf.

At the seaside the architect usually finds ideal sites for short holes staring him in the face, and he has to allow the lengths to be governed by the character of the ready-made hazards and the run of the ground. This applies to some extent at inland places, but here he often has to come to the assistance of Nature by contributing bunkers to her work, so that he has more scope for deciding as to what kind of shot shall be necessary from the tee. One hole may well be a mashie shot, measuring from 80 to 120 yards, and two others can be from 120 to 160 yards each in length, so as to give the man who is fond of his iron a chance of doing something good with it. These holes ought to present many difficulties without being unfair; the bunkers should be close in to the green, and capable of punishing anything in the nature of a bad stroke. Two other

holes may be of the full-shot variety (perhaps
some people will object to these being called
short holes, although, in any case, they are not
long), but here the bunkers guarding the front of
the green should be about twenty-five yards short
of the near edge of the putting area so as to allow
for the run which is inseparable from a full shot.
It is highly important, too, that the ground
between the bunker and the green should be as
good as Nature and humanity can combine to
make it. There should be no chance for it to
impart a kick to the ball. You know directly
you have played the tee shot whether you have hit
it well or ill, and it is bitterly disappointing to
see a good stroke kick into a bunker. When you
play to come in one way, it is annoying in the
extreme to see the ball jump the other way
through a fault in the fairway—or, in this case,
unfairway.

Gorse, bracken, and other flora of the heath or
common, stretching from teeing-ground to green,
constitute good guards for short holes, but where
it is necessary to dig a bunker, I need scarcely
say that the outline of the hazard should be, in
this case, more or less at right angles to the line
of play since there can only be one correct spot
to carry, even though that spot vary from day to
day, according to the wind. The diagonal
bunker comes into use at the longer holes. Of
these, the hardest to play under modern conditions
are, I think, those which measure about 400 yards,
and have well-protected greens. A good drive is
needed in any case; and against the wind, a full
second shot is often demanded. Still, a first-class
player can get home by means of two perfect
shots, and regain the stroke which he is giving to
an inferior opponent. I firmly believe in having a
bunker in front of the green with the object of

making the golfer play for the carry, which is the true game; but the hazard should be about forty yards short of the pin. In dry weather it is often wellnigh impossible to make the ball stop within a few yards of where it alights.

Five of these holes are not too many, and to give the shorter driver a periodical land of promise, I would have four holes of from 330 to 370 yards each. A distance of 330 yards is often described as bad, because, under normal circumstances, it requires more than one full shot and less than two strenuous strokes. But approaching is now by far the most difficult part of the game, and as recovery ought to be possible at any part of the course, there is no harm in occasionally facilitating it. With the cross-hazard existing to punish the poor drive, the person who had been guilty of a downright bad tee shot would have to effect an almost superhuman recovery to obtain a 4.

The gradient of the ground and the nature of the turf are often such as to decide definitely whether the green ought to be protected in front or left open. The unguarded entrance is good in certain circumstances. If the ground within, say, forty yards of the hole, slopes from either left or right towards the other side of the fairway, the approach is as difficult as any bunker could make it. The running shot will not take the slope properly unless you play it with slice or pull, according to whether the incline is from the right or the left, while to pitch over all of the thought-provoking slant and stop near the hole, calls for a very fine shot indeed.

We have now fixed upon fourteen holes, and the remaining four might measure anything from 420 to 580 yards. I do not think that any hole need run to 600 yards; as a rule, the very long

c

hole affords no better entertainment (perhaps not such good fun) as hitting a ball across Hyde Park—if anybody has tried the latter diversion. At the 500-yard test, I would not have a hazard rearing its menacing face at the player as he stood upon the teeing-ground.   Here—and here alone —he might be allowed to use every device in his power to obtain distance, untrammelled by the thought of bunkers ahead.   I would put the first cross-bunker about 360 yards from the tee.   If he could drive into that, he would be a martyr to his greatness and the dry ground.   Nor would I worry particularly about piling up trouble in front of the green; the prodigious driver could let himself go at this kind of hole.   But he would have to keep straight, and the open gateway to the green would not be expansive.

We have now a course comprising four more or less clearly defined types of holes (nicely assorted, let us hope) and giving a total distance of about 6,200 yards, which, I venture to say, is long enough for anybody.   It is impossible, I know, for this system of architecture to be put into force as one might measure off perches of ground, but its general principles are capable of adoption, and they are offered as the best that I can conceive in the modern conditions of golf. They tend to promote the true sport.   I have no sympathy with the encouragement of the flat, running shot for the long game.   It is neither more nor less than a subterfuge.

And now for a few general details.   Except at short holes, or where short approaches constitute the natural sequence to good drives, I would have the back of the green guarded only at a respectful distance—say, from ten to fifteen yards beyond the hole.   It is a good thing to tempt a player to go boldly for the pin, and he is apt to become frightened (and reasonably so) when he knows that the slightest excess of courage may bring irretrievable disaster upon his head. It is a great compliment to pay to a course to say that it encourages bold approaching. The green which is closely hemmed on all sides by bunkers and which, in the distance, looks hardly big enough to accommodate a foursome, may inspire skilful iron play in some instances, but it is much more likely to generate a spirit of timidity among golfers. So, without being indulgent, let us take care to be fair in regard to the amount of room that we leave at the back of the hole. Better is it to leave too much than too little.

The flanks of every green, as of the fairway, should be literally bestrewn with difficulties. There is some excuse for a rubber-cored ball going farther than we had intended it to go; but there is no excuse for its travelling crookedly. Rough—so long as it really is rough—is a greater embarrassment than almost any bunker. It is usually possible to see at a glance exactly how one will attempt to play a shot out of a bunker, but a ball in the rough often gives cause for deep cogitation. So let there be plenty of trouble on the wings—bunkers as well as other agents of distress. And, at this point, I should like to express the opinion that the punishment ought to be as severe for the puller as for the slicer. For some reason, the sentiment has grown up in golf that pulling is not nearly so heinous an offence as slicing. I cannot see any justification for such a judgment. It is wrong to be off the course on either side, and it is no less wrong to be off it on the left than on the right. Yet I have played on many links where, apparently, care had been taken not to severely punish the puller, while the slicer had been afforded enormous scope for working out his salvation in a region of sand and unpolished country.

It is desirable from every point of view that the course should be made to look as natural as possible. The position of your hazard is a matter of calculation inspired by a good knowledge of the game; the contour of it must be governed by a sense of artistry. The shape of the hazard may not be of great intrinsic importance, for it is just as bad to lose a stroke in a little pot bunker, precise in its roundness, as it is to suffer a similar set-back in the rugged magnificence of a mighty sand-hill. But while I have put in a plea for the restoration of the cross-bunker because it would revive the true golfing shot, I certainly would not suggest a revival of the ribbon bunkers which, ten years ago, stretched across courses in deadly dull straight lines, very prim and prosaic in their pattern. A chain of three or four fairly large pot bunkers, with ragged and irregular outlines, is often more pleasing to the eye than a continuous hazard from side to side. And it is just as effective. So, too, in regard to the guarding of the green.

Pot bunkers scattered here and there just off the line are good, because they exercise an extraordinary magnetism on the golfer, and it should be his duty to overcome that influence. An instance which I have in mind is the pot on the way to the ninth at St Andrews. It is no bigger than a dining-room table, but the number of shots that go into it is amazing. For inland clubs, the great drawback to the system of bunkering which I have put forward is the cost of sand. It is an expensive luxury, and at many places the exchequer will not permit of repeated renewals of the supplies which errant golfers have scattered to the winds. But there is much to be said for grassy hazards—punishing places of much the same size and shape as bunkers, but with rough ground instead of sand as the fundamental feature. Rough, as I have already said, is harder to get out of than sand. The one objection to grassy hazards is that they are apt to become wet in the winter, but, if the ground be properly drained, they need be little, if any, worse than the other parts of the course.

Still, sand is the proper foundation of a bunker, and where the latter is dug and shaped by the hand of man, I would advance a principle which is all too often ignored. Frequently one finds the expanse of hazard practically level with the fairway, while a bulwark of earth rises on the far side of the bunker like a rampart that has been built in defence of a fort. This may be satisfactory enough as a test for the tee shot, but it is not the proper kind of bunker for the approach. It is usually almost as simple to dig down on the near side and allow the bottom of the bunker to slope up gradually to the level of the green. The player then has a sight of the hole, no matter from what distance he is approaching. This uninterrupted vision is important, because it is almost impossible to tell, by merely catching a glimpse of the flag, the length of shot required. There is a lot of flukiness about aiming at the flag. The golfer presented with a semi-blind approach will do well to go forward until he can see the pin at the point where it enters the ground.

The mounds which have become so popular during the past year or two are good so long as they possess the correct features. A club which had decided to adopt this means of relieving the monotony of a flat course could not do better than work on the plan of the originators, the Mid-Surrey Club. Many clubs have introduced mounds of the wrong kind, with steep faces, which make the ball dart off at any angle, sometimes for good and on other occasions for ill, and which present a general appearance of unnaturalness, as though a number of earthen cones had been purchased and dotted about the course. Another point worthy of attention is the desirability of having undulating putting-greens instead of flat ones. Nowadays, there is a disposition in many places to make a green as much as possible like a billiard table, but it is not conducive to good putting. I fear that I possess—and deserve—a most unenviable reputation as a holer-out, but I know that I can generally putt better when I have to "borrow" some ground to allow for a slope than when the stroke is perfectly straightforward. The reason is, I think, that the sloping green makes the player ponder, whereas on a flat green he is prone to come to the conclusion that there is not much to consider. And concentration of the mind is the surest means to successful putting. There is no other royal road to triumph.

This, then, is my idea of a good course for modern golf. It should make the player revert to the old desire to obtain the longest possible carry from the tee, and then he will soon discover how to play the lofted approach with an iron club—the shot which has almost disappeared from the game, and the disappearance of which has done so much to lower the standard of play. We can make golf nearly as good a game as it used to be if we secure the right kind of hazards, and check the craze for the running shot, which the rubber-cored ball incited and which, in many places, has been deliberately encouraged by the abandonment of cross-bunkers.

CHAPTER III

EQUIPMENT: SOME TRIFLES THAT AMOUNT TO MUCH

GOLF is a strange game: it enchants and aggravates, it flatters and disappoints, it rears up the player to believe in his efficiency and then lets him down with a clash. It is a kind of kaleidoscope interrupted at intervals by nightmares. It no sooner elevates its devotee than it dispirits him; it no sooner dispirits him than it elates him. That is the secret of its seductiveness, and at the back of it all is an illimitable vista of hope. The unquenchable consolation of the golfer's life is that if this or the other means fail him in his quest of success, he can try other media. To the player who is in the throes of incapacity with a certain club, a new implement is ethereal; it holds out unbounded promise. I suppose that nowhere is there a golfer—good, bad, or indifferent—who feels that he will never light on better instruments for the purpose of hitting the ball than those which he already possesses. In times of blackest despair, he sees salvation through an avenue of shafts and heads. I know of an open champion who, at the beginning of a season, abandoned every one of the clubs that had served him well for years, and equipped himself with an entirely fresh set. He had not been satisfied with his game for some months, and he wanted to start life again.

That is the best of a new club; it seems to mark the beginning of a new career. The idea may be pure imagination, but imagination has a practical value in golf. Faith-cures are everyday dispensations of Providence. Give a player a club which he has never previously used, and which he fancies from top to sole, and he will often do great things with it, for no better reason than that he likes it. He is filled with the sentiment that it is the deliverer for which he has been searching for months, and that is sufficient to enable him to improve his results.

Experience alone teaches a golfer what clubs suit him best; it is only when he has been playing for some time that he begins to wonder whether he is handicapping himself by using unsuitable instruments. At the outset, he may go to a shop and purchase a brassie, an iron, a mashie, and a putter. He takes hold of them; and flourishes them; yes; they appear to be all right. He comes away happy. He takes his first lesson, and is perhaps told to grip them differently from the way in which he held them in the shop. Then it is that their beauties begin to vanish. In a little while they become monsters of ungainliness and discomfort. They seem to be dragging his hands down; they are either too long or too short; too thick or too thin; they are abortions. The absolute beginner cannot do better than borrow an old club from a professional, and discover his natural stance, length of swing, and other individualities before he proceeds to purchase a set of implements. The professional will be able to tell him at the end of ten minutes what sort of tools will suit him best.

Let us assume, however, that we are dealing

with the case of the player who already has his
outfit, and who is concerned with the question
as to whether it is the best that the resources of
the club-making trade can provide for his benefit.
The frequency with which one sees a golfer using
wooden instruments of different degrees of " lie "
is extraordinary. Everybody must find out for
himself what " lie " of the club he likes best;
the choice varies even amongst champions. As
a rule, it should be in the nature of a happy
medium; neither too upright nor too flat; for the
rest, personal fancies may well govern the selection. But having lighted on the " lie " which
makes him feel confident when he uses---let us
say—the driver, the player should take care to
have the same " lie " in his brassie. Yet how
often a difference exists! In many cases, it is
the cause of that despairing cry—" Hang it!
I shall never be able to use a brassie! " The
unfortunate bungler through the green is adopting the same stance and the same swing and trying to play the same sort of shot with two clubs
that have practically nothing in common. If he
has an " upright " driver and a " flat " brassie
and stands the same for both, as he is nearly sure
to do, only the toe of the brassie will be touching the turf when he addresses the ball. Or,
with the " lie " of the implements transposed,
only the heel of the brassie will be grounded
during the address. He might overcome the difficulty by altering his stance for each club, but it
would be a pity to make a necessity of such a
change when he could avoid it by having a driver
and a brassie of similar build.

I presume that most golfers appreciate the
fact that the shaft of the driver ought to be a
little more whippy than that of the brassie. I do
not mean to suggest that the former should have

the pliability of a cane, but it is indisputable that a certain amount of "feel" in it facilitates the swing. The driver does not come into contact with the ground during the execution of a tee shot (at any rate, it should not), so that a reasonable element of suppleness cannot operate adversely. And it certainly renders the swing pleasanter and stronger. The brassie needs a slightly heavier and stiffer shaft because it has to cut through the grass; in bad lies, it even has to take some turf. A whippy shaft in a brassie would be disastrous, because it would bend when it came to blows with the earth. Sometimes, in ripe old age the club develops from constant use some degree of liveliness. We do not like to part with a trusted friend, especially when it happens to comprise a really excellent shaft, but it is as well to be on the look out for this tendency to sprightliness on the part of the brassie of long service, and it is often a good tip to have it converted into a driver. Frequently it has just the right amount of "feel" in it for the purpose.

Be it remembered that the driver in constant use is apt to become in course of time too supple. It is employed probably four or five times more than the brassie, and the busy life that it leads causes it to develop a lot of springiness. The keen golfer should pause occasionally to consider this matter; it is of some importance. He should note the changing characteristics of his clubs, especially the wooden ones, which, owing to the greater delicateness of their shafts, are more likely to alter than the iron-headed tools.

It is always as well to carry two drivers—one fairly stiff and the other moderately supple. There are times when you are convinced that you can hit anything—from an ant to a golf ball. Your spirits are so high that you feel that the whole world is at your mercy on the links. A man in this state of exhilaration is frequently shocked to find that, when he begins playing, the shots do not come off very well after all. The reason is usually to be found in his exuberance. He is so filled with natural fire that he cannot swing with measured regularity; he is so replete with confidence that he takes the club back like lightning. Then is the time to use the stiff driver. It will act as a brake on his excessive hilarity; it will hold him in check; it simply will not be whirled out of its tautness. When the golfer is subdued, and is swinging in a decorous manner, let him use the more whippy shaft. Then it will help him. It will put life into his golf. The truth of these observations I have proved to my own satisfaction on many occasions. It is one of the best of hints to carry two drivers. The frequency with which one will prove friendly when the other has become peevish is astonishing. The explanation is to be found, I think, in the theory that the difference in the whippiness operates in connexion with the variations in the pace of the swing. None of us swing at just the same speed every day.

These are points to which professionals are always giving attention; they are matters well worthy of consideration. It is only natural that professionals should inquire into such matters more deeply than amateurs; the former have their livelihood to obtain by means of their golf They have to think of every possibility, and probe deeply into the questions of cause and effect. An amateur lives in a land of hope which either realizes expectations or proves barren. When he is off his driving—well, he is off his driving. There, as a rule, the matter rests. He does not often ruminate as to the reason. It seldom occurs to him that the pace of his swing may be doing the mischief, and that, if he has only one driver in his bag, no rule can prevent him from trying his brassie for the tee shots.

Professionals have long since come to the conclusion that the wooden clubs used by many indifferent players are too long. It is easier to control a short driver than a long one; with the former, you have your nose to the grindstone, so to speak, and seem to be in a condition of better concentration for the task than with an implement of unwieldy length. Still I have no desire to be dogmatic on the point. There are people who can control long clubs; it must be rather difficult work, but they are capable of performing it. That being so, they may be allowed to play in peace.

Iron clubs should be stiff; they should have no " give " in them at all that the player can distinguish. They have to at least graze the turf every time, often they have to go into the soil in order to get behind the ball. And it is certain that excavation on even the most modest scale cannot be properly carried out with a tool that bends. There are heretics who, at this point, may come up for the humble judgment of a conscientious golfer. They are the people who use nothing but irons, even from the tee. They are not only unorthodox and blind to their own interests; they are faint-hearted. They think that they cannot master wooden clubs, and they have not the courage to make a determined effort to do so. They seek to evade the difficulties of the game by accomplishing their tee shots with a driving mashie or kindred instrument. They will never make good players, and they will never know the full joy of the links.

In the case of a golfer of some experience, instinct is the best adviser in the choice of a club. As you take the creation in your hands, you can generally tell at once whether it is just the thing that you have been wanting for a long while. This, I know, is a commonly accepted truth; yet there are players who judge largely by the appearance of the implement. Looks are often deceiving; they ought to have no influence in the making of the final selection. A club that is by no means pleasing to the eye is sometimes found to be the best of the bunch when the prospector tries the "feel" of it. Yet many a golfer passes it by because its looks are against it. Lancewood makes a very pretty shaft; people are apt to be immensely impressed by its aspect. It is certainly the most handsome of all woods employed in connexion with clubmaking; but personally I would not recommend its use. It has the advantage of stiffness, but it is too heavy for iron clubs, and the same drawback in the matter of excessive weight renders it a difficult wood with which to make a brassie of pleasant "feel" and balance. Some of the weight can be removed by filing down the shaft towards the head, but the result is not always happy. In addition, it is so hard a wood that, in the case of a driver or a brassie, there is difficulty in inducing the shaft and the head to remain in adherence. Lancewood has a soul above adhesive substances; it declines to allow glue to bite it with the requisite strength. One does not see a lot of it, and I fear that it will never satisfactorily solve problems that may be presented by a famine of other woods. So long as we can obtain good hickory for our shafts, we ought to be glad.

Golf is made up of details, and it is the player

who considers all the small points who succeeds in the end. The correct swing performed with suitable clubs constitutes three-quarters of the battle; when both sides have the capacity and the equipment here indicated, the victory goes to the man who gives the greater amount of thought to matters of seemingly minor importance. Let us take, for instance, the preparations on the teeing-ground. A first-class golfer is often seen shifting uneasily for several seconds about this confined area, apparently searching for a nice piece of grass on which to build a tee. I know that thousands of people imagine that he is hunting for such a spot. They must marvel at his fastidiousness, and thank Providence that they have not become so well-known as to justify such affectation. But the good golfer is not so silly as to want a choice square inch of turf on which to deposit a little sand. He is simply feeling with his feet for a comfortable stance. There is only one stage in the playing of each hole where he has such a choice, and he makes the most of it. That he is looking at the ground all the while is due to the fact that it would, in any case, be rather silly to gaze into the faces of the spectators or up to the heavens. The difference between an easy stance and an uneasy one on the teeing-ground often means the difference between a good drive and a bad one. Yet I am certain that a great many golfers really do hunt for a dainty piece of grass on which to make a tee, although its importance compared with that of a pleasant stance is hardly worth considering. Often, too, a player is seen re-teeing his ball because he finds that he cannot settle down properly in the place which he has selected. The change is disturbing. It is better to obtain the right spot at the outset.

Very few caddies make good tees. The ball
should be just perched on the sand so that none
of the latter can be seen; the ball should seem
to be sitting up clear of the ground, supported
by nothing. That optical delusion gives you confidence to hit it well; the eye is not attracted by
the presence of a setting. Often a player who
wants a lower tee will give the top of the ball
a knock and so push it into the sand. I honestly
believe that many shots are spoilt in that way;
you cannot always obtain in such circumstances
the stroke that would be secured with the per-
fectly-poised ball. There are men who, at times,
almost bunker themselves in the tee. The less
sand that you have for the purpose, the richer
will be the ultimate reward.

The reader who likes to take his golf in a
spirit of light-hearted irresponsibility may come
to the conclusion that in offering these hints I
am reducing instruction to a very fine point. I
can only assure him that the best players owe
much of their success to their attention to small
details, and that if his temperament be such that
he cannot bother to hunt for a good stance when
he is allowed a choice, or concern himself about
the character of his tee, he will probably remain
in possession of a handicap of more or less considerable proportions. Not that careful consideration of these matters will alone suffice to make
him a good golfer (the game would be very
easy if a perfect tee meant a perfect drive), but
they will train him to be careful in his attitude
towards the whole pursuit, and I am sure that
nobody can fare well on the links without thinking hard all the while—reflecting on the cause
of his wrong-doings and the best way of putting
them right. Golf is a monument composed of
small items—the very swing is made up of details,

each important for the production of the desired
end.

Apart from the matter of obtaining a comfortable stance, it frequently pays the golfer to consider from which side of the teeing-ground he
shall drive. Yet how many players bother about
such a point? Very few. The majority select
a spot somewhere near the middle of the space
between the discs. Yet, if you have an out-of-
bounds area on either the right or the left, it is
surely a sound idea to make your tee as far as
possible from that evil region. " Out of bounds "
exercises a sort of magnetic influence on many
an indifferent golfer; it seems to coax him to hit
his ball into it. He knows that it is there; that
is the whole secret of its power over him. He
may help to remove himself from the zone of its
influence by starting from a point as far from it
as the limits of the teeing-ground will permit.
If you are playing for an intentional slice, it is
always best, I think to tee up on the right-hand
side of the starting-place, because you have then
more room into which to aim. It is necessary
to aim at an unseen point in the air; there is
just one point, you feel, at which the wind should
hold up the ball, and enter into the conspiracy
with the slice to bring the object back to the
course. You can see that point more clearly when
you are playing out to it than when you are going
almost straight at it. Similarly, for a pulled
shot, it is desirable to begin on the left-hand
side of the teeing-ground.

Personally, I recommend thin grips for all
clubs. I tried thick grips for a short time; but
did not get on at all well with what I called my
" cricket bats." They were a desperate remedy
that proved worse than the disease. Nor do I
believe in the specially-shaped grips which are

made to fit the fingers. At first blush, the idea of such a handle seems excellent. Why should the grip be round? Why should it not be of such a shape as to guide the hand to the proper position on the club? I have experimented with these devices, and my experience of them is that they succeed so effectually in their object that they render gripping far too easy. They so greatly facilitate the task that there is little about which to think, and, as a result, they encourage a vice-like hold. They are so simple to grasp that one instinctively grasps them tightly—much too tightly—with all the fingers. The ordinary round grip is less accommodating, and, as a consequence, it induces the player to consider just what he is doing. I am convinced that it is bad to have the shape of the handle so inviting to the fingers that they involuntarily grip it like grim death. And that is the drawback to various innovations that have made their appearance in connexion with golf-club handles.

From small and often unconsidered sources, great assistance is obtainable. For instance, man is lucky in his right to wear braces so long as he wear the right sort of braces. They should be trained by use to work in harmony with the swing of the player; they should become to all intents and purposes part of that swing. Then they will help it and control it. I would no more think of going out to play for a championship in a new pair of braces than of trying to do the four rounds on my head. I should not know how to swing. Nearly every professional of note has his braces that fit all his movements, and they are treasured possessions. They may not look very smart, but he would not exchange them for the most exquisite creation that could be brought to bear upon his shoulders. There

D

is nothing worse than having to teach proper golfing manners to a new pair of braces. Some players prefer belts The latter, I think, give the shoulders too much freedom, and encourage the fatal fault of overswinging. Braces are best, but they must be on friendly terms with their owner.

Whether you wear boots or shoes should be governed in a large degree by the extent to which you use your ankles when playing. I would certainly recommend a beginner to support the cult of shoe worship, because his early studies may well be directed towards the learning of how to screw the left ankle properly. And shoes will render the task easier. If, having mastered the knack, he finds his fancy turning lightly towards boots, I have not the smallest desire to dissuade him from effecting the change. Braid and Taylor always play in boots. Personally, I prefer shoes; I make a lot of use of my ankles, and like them free. In any case, very thick soles are bad. As the left foot twists from the joints of the big toe during the upward swing, the boot or shoe should be prepared to " give " a little. The foot should not be encased as though in a vice. If you cannot screw your left ankle into the proper position without pushing your heel out, it is possible that the sole of your boot or shoe is too substantial. There is not much " give " in a massive chunk of leather.

Collars are by no means unimportant details of dress. It is as well to have something round your neck for appearance's sake, but it is bad when that something stands two inches or more in height. I can assure the reader that most of the professionals have their collars specially made for them. They are an inch high. I mean, of course that the collars are an inch high—not the professionals. Often one sees a golfer playing in neck-gear of enormous dimensions. As he takes the club back the chances are that the collar forces his head to one side, and the fatal habit of swaying is encouraged. The bottom of your neck has to screw with the body while the head remains still, and a high collar upsets the whole scheme.

I have nothing to say on the burning question of trousers versus knickerbockers, except that the latter facilitate that freedom of the ankle and leg which is so desirable. I have no particular pattern of tie to suggest; in fact, I am finished with the subject of clubs and clothes. I have not been hypercritical in compiling this chapter of hints. I have learnt from experience that each of the points hereinmentioned may be worth a stroke at some time or other. And a stroke often means the difference between winning a hole and only halving it.

CHAPTER IV

TWO ESSENTIALS OF SUCCESS

EARLY in this book the statement is made that, under present-day conditions, it is comparatively easy to enjoy a fair measure of success on the links. In the abstract, the declaration is perhaps more cheery than convincing. I do not wish it to be taken as meaning that to reach the loftiest heights of golfing fame is a simple matter. To become a first-class golfer still requires much patient study. During recent years, however, the game has become the outstanding recreation of busy men, and they usually insist that they do not want to waste their precious hours of leisure in taking lessons and practising the same shot time after time. They want to get out on to the course, and have a match with somebody. It is not too much to say that a new class of golfers has arisen since the arrival of the rubber-cored ball. It numbers thousands of people, and they are chiefly conspicuous for the extreme carelessness with which they play their shots—carelessness which has been born, I suppose, of the knowledge that the ball is often very kind to the bad player. Many of them declare that all they desire is exercise, and that they do not mind how badly they shape as golfers.

They generally express these sentiments when they stand about six down with five to play, and the match is over. Probably there are very few golfers devoid of ambition to make headway at the pastime, but undoubtedly there are many who feel that it would be a frittering away of time to take lessons, when they might be contesting some exciting games. The ease with which the ball can be persuaded a considerable distance has generated a spirit of heedlessness. This type of golfer is very unwise, because a short course of tuition at the outset of his golfing career might have been the means of giving him victory on numerous occasions when defeat has been his portion. On almost every course one sees many people who are clear examples of early neglect. They hold the club wrongly; in fact, they do nearly everything wrongly. And yet they marvel at the absence of appreciable improvement at the end of six months of golf.

They constitute such a numerous section of the community that I may here bring out a few points which should be of assistance to them in the correction of their faults. It has been said that there are ninety-nine things to remember while playing a stroke, and that the disregard of any one of them is sure to spoil the effort. To the golfer who is in the throes of a long novitiate, and who is at a loss to understand his or her repeated failure and protracted absence of progress, I say that there are just two primary and all-important points to remember. They are to grip the club properly and to keep the head steady. Master those two difficulties, and you are certain to advance in some degree. Most of the bad golf that is played is attributable to either a wrong method of holding the club or the moving of the head. There are other things to be learnt later, but to succeed in these two essentials is to place oneself well on the road to progress. To ignore them is to render progress practically impossible.

Of the two, perhaps the more important is the preservation, until the ball has been struck, of steadiness of the head. Directly that necessary nuisance starts to move with the club during the upward swing, the body begins to sway and is thrown out of gear and off its balance. The result is almost inevitably a bad shot. Amongst first-class players there are a few exceptions to the rule, and I sometimes think that they know more about the game than anybody else. They know so much about it that they are able to fly in the face of several established principles of the correct golfing style, and yet perform satisfactorily on the links. They are a law unto themselves.

For the old axiom. "Keep your eye on the ball," I would substitute, "Keep your head still," because, by performing the latter act of restrainment, you give the eye little chance to wander, which it certainly should not do, and you obtain the additional advantage of rendering comparatively easy the proper turn of the body. Directly you move the head, everything starts to go wrong. The body begins to sway and to prepare for a kind of lunge at the ball; and lunging, in the generally accepted sense of the word, is generally useless in golf. The action, to produce consistent success, must be that of swinging, with a certain element of hitting introduced in order to make for power.

This may be an elementary truth, known to and appreciated by many thousands of players; but I cannot help thinking that there are thousands of others who either have not heard it or do not realize its importance. It is astonishing how many people fall into an incorrect style, and render practically impossible the execution of a good shot ere they have taken the club-head a yard from the ball. The player's head moves in the same direction as the club, the body goes with it, as it would have to do unless the performer possessed a neck of india-rubber; and then all is over bar the imprecation of subdued disappointment.

Undoubtedly, however, there are very many golfers who know the value of the rule, and who think they are keeping their heads still when all the while they are doing nothing of the kind. Indeed, these constitute the majority. Often, during a course of instruction, the professional remarks at the end of a stroke, "You mustn't move your head," only to receive the almost indignant reply, "Well, I'm sure I didn't move it that time." The pupil is convinced that he has fulfilled the requirement to the last letter, and it is sometimes very difficult to convince him that he has not done so. His belief is whole-hearted. All the same, the intelligent instructor knows exactly what is wrong, and he can only possess his soul in patience as he says, "Now try again; and be sure you keep your head still." Enthusiasts have adopted truly noble and desperate measures in order to master this necessity. There was once a man who tied his head to a tree as a means of teaching it a lesson. Whenever it received a jerk—and some of the jerks must have been almost sufficient to dislocate his neck—he knew that he had committed the old error. There was another player who thought of a highly ingenious device. I understand that to a button on his waistcoat he affixed a piece of elastic—not securely, but with just sufficient firmness that a

real tug at it would pull it off the button. The
other end he held tightly in his teeth so that the
elastic was moderately taut without being severely
stretched. Then he set his teeth with great good
purpose and made his swing. His theory was
that if the elastic jumped off the button and
smacked him in the face, he would know that
he had moved his head. Unfortunately he had
forgotten that his body would move with his
head.

There was another player who, in order to overcome his inclination to spread his arms too far
apart, introduced a thick india-rubber band, which
he fixed from elbow to elbow. Those trouble-
some members were thereby prevented from
going wrong in the outward direction. The only
danger to which they were submitted was that of
getting too close together. The arms, however,
constitute a secondary consideration; we are talk-
ing now of the head, the steadiness of which is
the first desideratum. I do not suppose that many
players would feel inclined to tether themselves
to trees in order to correct their faults; but I
have seen a little device, as simple as it is clever,
which is certainly the most masterly means ever
conceived of drilling a golfer in the matter of
head-restraint. It is so very simple that I cannot help wondering why nobody thought of
it years ago. It does not cause the smallest
inconvenience. It cannot even be seen by
the player as he swings, and yet it tells him
instantly whether he has moved his head or
accomplished the all-important task of keeping
it still.

At first, the golfer may be inclined to smile
when I describe to him this contrivance. I can
only assure him that I have tried it for the benefit of several players, and that the results have

always been excellent. I do not claim any credit for the idea. It was conceived by Colonel Quill, who took up golf at the age of fifty-six, and, with the help of his corrector, made himself a scratch player in eighteen months. I find that with most people who start golf fairly late in life (at any rate after the age of forty) the commonest difficulty is that of keeping the head steady. Especially is this the case amongst persons who have not kept in more or less athletic condition by pursuing cricket or some other pastime. Their bodies become set, and they find it a very trying matter to turn at the waist, more particularly if they happen to have a lot of waist to turn. All the same, they must learn to do so if they would acquire any proficiency at all; it is the only way to secure success at golf. If they do not turn, they generally move the body and head away from the ball since they must make some backward movement in preparation for the onslaught. That is where they go wrong. It is the fault which they must never give up trying to cure.

Let me describe the device of Colonel Quill. Let me explain, too, the way in which he made it. He obtained a hollow brass post, about three feet long. Truth to tell, it was a bedpost. One end he fashioned to a point, so that it could be stuck into the ground. Down the post, from within about a foot of the top to within a few inches of the bottom, he made a narrow incision in the metal—a gap about a quarter of an inch wide. Some strong thread, a small piece of tin, and a fish-hook completed the articles of manufacture. The thread was slipped through the post, and to the end of it was affixed the piece of tin so that the latter rested outside the upright. The other end of the thread was sufficiently long to reach to the cap of the player as he stood in proper position for a shot. It was fixed to the cap by the fish-hook.

All this may seem somewhat weird, but as to the value of the instrument I have not the slightest doubt. It is an extraordinarily effective means of practice for the indifferent golfer—or even the good one who finds that he is doing badly and knows not quite why. Lessons and hints from a human instructor are none the less desirable, but this contrivance enables the player to decide, when shots do not come off in practice as they ought to do, whether or not he is moving his head, which is the fault productive of most bad strokes.

Let us assume that the aspirant is at work with one of these posts. He takes up his stance, the thread being stretched, with perhaps an inch of slackness permitted, from his cap to the piece of tin at the bottom of the upright. He cannot see any part of his training-machine because his eyes are fixed on the ball. He swings. What happens? If he moves his head the metal indicator begins to run up the post, tinkling merrily the while. It affords irrefutable evidence against him. In effect, it shouts to him the instant he starts to make the old mistake: "Hi! you're shifting your head," and it is not the smallest use for him to protest t:_ he is doing nothing of the kind. He stands convicted by the tinkle, and when he hears it, there is little object in his continuing the stroke, for, with his head moving, there is but a poor chance of the shot being a good one. He must settle down to the task of working out his salvation by practising and practising until he can make full swings without stirring the indicator. When he can do that, he has mastered the greatest difficulty that golf presents to the average beginner. There are, of course, other things that he may do wrongly, but they are generally capable of easier remedy than this first and most frequent fault. The chances are that he has now acquired the way of turning properly from the waist and thus distributing his weight properly. I have submitted Colonel Quill's simple contrivance to many tests. I have tried full swings and followed through to the fullest extent. When I have been playing well, there has been no suspicion of a tug at the thread and consequently no warning note from the indicator. In all sincerity, I say that it is the best form of preparation that I know for an indifferent player who suffers from the common failing, and who wants to improve. If he cannot go to the links more than twice a week, he can practise swings in his garden, or even in the house if his ingenuity be such as to enable him to induce the contrivance to stand on the floor. In these limited areas, he cannot be sure—unless he use a captive ball—whether he is topping or even missing the globe altogether, but if his efforts leave the metal undisturbed, he can rest assured that he is getting into the way of the true golfing swing.

I have given foremost position to this matter of keeping the head still, because the neglect of it is the cause of so much bad golf, but, as mentioned earlier in this chapter, it is absolutely necessary that the club should be gripped in the proper way. In a sense, there are two proper ways. There is the old-fashioned grip, in which the hands meet on the shaft of the club but do not overlap, and there is the overlapping grip, which, personally, I think is by far the better and which is now adopted by nearly every professional of note. These, however, are both two V grips, in the sense that the thumb and forefinger form V's down the shaft of the club.

So that here we come to the first important
point concerning the grip. It is that, whether the
hands overlap or not, the thumbs and forefingers
must be placed so as to shape into V's. Sometimes you see players holding a club as they might
seize a rope for a tug-of-war. They place the implement deeply in the palms, and the knuckles are
almost hidden from view beneath the shaft. That
style is bound to be fatal, because, in order to
take the club right back, it becomes necessary
to loosen the grip with all the fingers. And such
loosening must inevitably weaken the shot. If,
then, you decide to employ the old-fashioned grip,
it is necessary to have the two V's in evidence,
and it is even more important to remember to
keep the hands wedged well together. If you
separate them only a little, it is the same as having
a club in each hand, the one trying to do something different from the other.

This latter statement is an established fact, and
it is the desirability of having the hands contiguous
which constitutes the great recommendation of
the overlapping grip. For, with that method of
holding the club, the two hands become practically
one. They are wedded, and if the ceremony of
wedding them be properly performed and a little
forbearance be shown at the outset, when minor
discomforts may be experienced, I can promise
that they will live very happily together ever
after. The illustrations will perhaps convey the
idea of this grip better than I can explain it. The
simplest way to obtain it is to take the club in the
left hand, the shaft pressing into the top (or little)
joint of the forefinger. As the wrist should be
turned so as to show the knuckles, the thumb will
be urged past the shaft. Bring it back, and place
it down the shaft. We now have the left thumb
firmly on the club, and the top joint of the left

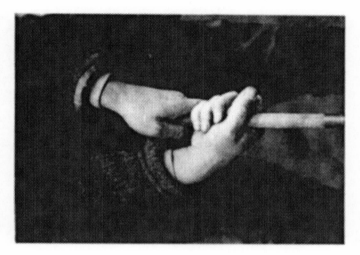

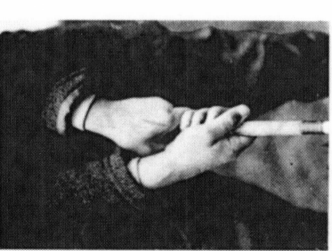

GRIPS RIGHT AND WRONG

The ordinary grip in which the hands touch but do not overlap. Amongst leading professionals it has been almost entirely superseded by the overlapping grip

A frequently seen but unquestionably wrong grip. The right wrist is bent, and the right hand is turned too far under the shaft. The effect will be a scoop rather than a hit

forefinger exercising a determined hold. It is with these two members that we want to grip tightest; that is why we are making use of the strongest part of the left forefinger. In the ordinary way, it is the finger with which we find we apply least pressure when we take hold of anything. It seems to be a law of Nature that the littler fingers shall be able to grip the more securely. Try them, for instance, when seizing a stick. In golf we want them to act chiefly as guides; their superior strength must be suppressed. Consequently, let the second, third and little fingers fall into natural position after a firm grip has been taken with the left thumb supported by the forefinger. In the case of the right hand, the ball of the thumb—that rounded protuberance of admirable proportions—is utilized to place over the left thumb, the top of which alone remains exposed to view. The first three fingers of the right hand clasp the shaft, and the little finger presses firmly on the forefinger of the left hand. Then the union is complete. I have heard people say that this grip is peculiarly suited to me because I am endowed with unusually long fingers. Personally, I think that fingers of more than the normal length are a handicap rather than a help, because one has to find room for them. Anybody can adopt this style of holding the club, and I think that everybody will agree that—theoretically at any rate—it is correct. It forms a perfect confederacy of the hands. I hesitate to say that there is a master hand in golf. A lot of people plump for the left. But the right hand should grip firmly; in fact there should be as little difference as possible. There is no need to press so hard as to make the blood run out of the hands, but in no circumstances should you permit any degree of slackness.

It took me a year of constant experimentation to satisfy myself as to the superiority of this grip over all others. I tried every conceivable means of holding the club, and the one which I have described proved itself to be indisputably the best. It did not come naturally to me, but it was well worth the trouble of acquiring. It seems to create just the right fusion between the hands, and involuntarily induces each to do its proper work.

For the beginner, there is no preparation so good as that of practising for a month or two without playing so much as a single complete round. If, after deciding to take up the game and getting the taste for blood which comes of the first few attempts to hit the ball—if, at this stage, he be capable of such splendid self-restraint as to spend all his time on the links during the ensuing six weeks in taking lessons from one qualified to teach and in practising what he has learnt, his progress will be rapid—far more so than that of the person who takes every opportunity to engage in a match. It is, I know, a counsel of perfection, but men have followed it, and, in an extraordinarily short time, have reached a fair measure of proficiency with the clubs which are called upon to do most of the work. Let the neophyte tackle them one by one without attempting fancy or complicated shots. All that he needs to do at the outset is to learn the proper grip, the way to keep the head steady, and the correct swing. The rest will come later, and the quality of it will depend largely on his inborn talent for the game and his opportunities for developing it. But he can usually learn to play tolerably well in a short time by the exercise of self-denial while he is studying the fundamental principles of the pastime. If he be incapable of

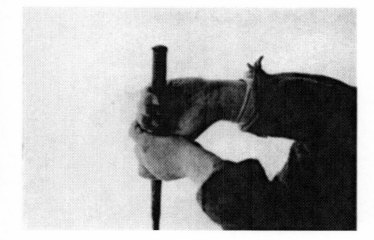

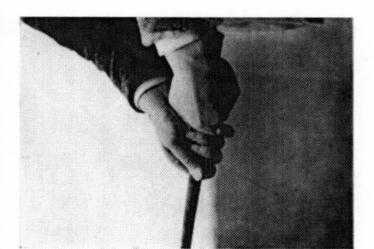

As seen at the beginning of the swing

THE OVERLAPPING GRIP

And at the top of the swing

such heroics, those principals will naturally take much longer in finding a place in his system. A person who starts wrongly and plays in the wrong manner for several months may prove to be a golfer lost. Salvation is a protracted and painful process when, in golf, a man has been following for some months a false trail.

CHAPTER V

HOW TO DRIVE

THE easiest strokes in golf are, I think, shots from the tee with a brassie and from the fairway with an iron. Therefore I would suggest to the beginner, or to the person who is almost resigned to mediocrity, that he should settle down at once to the task of mastering those shots. They are not difficult; but they are impossible unless the player knows how to swing the club properly. The golf swing is different from anything else in sport. It deserves to be called an art. There is only one way of executing it correctly. At least, that is true of its fundamental features. From time to time one hears and reads of various kinds of swings. Years ago, for instance, the talk was all of the St Andrews swing. That swing consists of sweeping the club round the legs until the arms will allow it to go no farther without moving the body, and then bringing the implement back in order to be able to raise it comfortably. To all intents and purposes, it is a matter of going out of the way and having to return to the right track. When the upward swing is three-quarters completed, the adept at the St Andrews method is on the same track as any other proficient golfer at the corresponding

64

stage of the ordinary swing. The latter has
simply gone straight to the point, while the
devotee of the St Andrews style has taken a
round-about route. Sometimes one hears of a
good player having a " flat swing." I venture
to say that if the swing is correct, it cannot be
" flat." Again, the expression means that the
player starts on a track which he must abandon.
A person who never soars above a half-swing
may certainly make it a " flat " one, but he will
not often be a good golfer.

I do not suggest that the aforementioned variations in the early part of the full swing are
necessarily fatal. What I do say is that they are
useless, and that, from three-quarters to the top,
and thence to the moment of impact, there is
only one proper course for the club-head to
follow, and that all accomplished players follow
it. It requires a genius to start on the wrong
track and get on to the right one.

There are people who declare that the perfect
way to learn golf is to learn it backwards. That
is to say, they advocate a scheme whereby the
beginner practises putting for a start, and works
his way by a kind of inverted curriculum—the
mashie, then the iron, then the cleek—until he
studies the full swing with wooden clubs.
At first blush, the idea may seem to have something to recommend it. For one thing, it is novel,
and a novelty generally possesses a degree of
charm. What, however, contributes most to the
plausibility of this plan is the fact that the player
is taught to hit the ball farther and farther and
make his swing longer and longer. There is an
appearance of logicality about the notion of beginning in a small way and gradually rising to
the glory of long hitting.

A little reflection, however, will show that such

E

reasoning is a delusion where the study of golf is concerned. If the short shots were easier than the long ones, it would be all right, but it so happens that approaching is about the most difficult part of the game. As for learning to putt first, I should imagine that anybody would become heartily sick of the business before he had half completed it. I do not know when a person can be said to have learnt putting. There are certain points well worth studying in connexion with it, but there is no infallible prescription for making the ball go into the hole every time—or even every other time. I wish I could discover one. In connexion with the full swing, there are golden rules which can be learnt, and the practice of which will produce success. And it is best, I think, to begin with shots for the practice of which there exist plenty of data.

Therefore, let the neophyte, or the player who fears that he is an incurably bad golfer, resolve to master first of all the way of executing a shot off the tee with his brassie. This is the easiest full shot in the realm of golf, and the accomplishment of it always affords a thrill of pleasure and encouragement. Moreover, once he has made himself proficient at it, the knowledge thus acquired will be a considerable help to him in playing the more difficult strokes. I suggest a brassie rather than a driver, because the former, having a slight loft on it, generates the greater amount of confidence. Moreover, as it is the less whippy of these two wooden clubs, it is the simpler to control. The methods of making a shot from the tee and a shot from a good lie on the course are—or should be—identical. The skilled golfer often employs his driver with great effect when the ball lies on the fairway, although, in such circumstances, it is perhaps a little

the more difficult club to wield satisfactorily.
The beginner cannot do better than seize
upon the easiest stroke of all, which is the
brassie shot from the tee. Once he is master of
it, he will find the driver joyous to use. The
two clubs being of the same length (it is important
to see that they do not vary in this respect), the
driver will be much the same in his hands as the
club with which he has been practising. The
troublesomeness of its straight face, which at the
the outset might have been considerable, will be
unrecognized now that he feels sure of hitting
the ball, and, what is equally important, he will
have made a friend of the brassie. The latter is
often regarded as the hardest club to use on the
fairway. That perhaps is only natural. On the
tee, the ball sits up temptingly, entreating a
strong blow. On the turf, it seems to be sitting
down, and there arises the necessity of picking
it up cleanly, and, at the same time, hitting it
with all the neatness and power that were inspired
by the sight of its shining face raised clear of
the ground. Therefore, the player is in every
respect well advised in getting on good terms at
once with his brassie. Let him have a low tee
(the lower, within reason, the better) and, in due
course, the driver will present no trouble to him,
and the brassie, when he takes it for a shot
through the green, will be an old friend. For,
as I have already said, the methods of using the
two clubs should, under favourable conditions,
be exactly the same. When the lie is unfavourable
there are certain variations which can be explained
later.

For the moment let us consider the swing. As
I have previously remarked, little can go wrong
if the grip be correct and the head be kept still.
The latter form of restraint is, for the ordinary

golfer, vital to the success of the stroke, and to the learner I can give no better advice than the hint to drill his head to preserve a state of rigidity by the use of that device conceived by Colonel Quill. Keeping the eye on the ball is important, and I do not suggest that anybody should forget it; but it is a secondary point. Keeping the head still is the prime essential. It is not much use having the vision fixed on the ball when the head is moving—except in the case of a first-class golfer who, when he shifts his head, knows how to recover during the swing. The stance must be easy and comfortable without undue stooping or any degree of stiffness. Ease and comfort are a lot. Just stand in an unconstrained way and address the ball by placing the club-head at the back of it, which is the proper part of the ball on which to fix your eye. It is the part to be hit.

I will not advance as a necessity any system of measurement. Of late years I have experimented a good deal with my own stance. Marking a certain spot for the tee, I have carefully noted the position of my feet before driving the ball. Then I have walked away, returned to the place and driven another ball from the same tee. I have repeated this operation four or five times, marking the position of my feet on each occasion, and in no two cases has the stance been precisely the same. There has not been much variation; yet every stance has been different from every other. So I will not ask the golfer to bother his head about mathematical calculations. Let us assume that he is standing comfortably upon the teeing-ground, addressing the ball. Let him remember that, except as regards the arms, the space which he now occupies ought to constitute the limit of his sphere of movement for that

shot. He must act in the area which he has
allotted to himself, because he wants to make not
a lunge at the ball, but a swing. Even the arms
return to that area and finish in it. If his feet
reach to either end of a sheet of newspaper, his
body ought not to move outside the ground
covered by that paper.

The golf swing is produced by twisting the
body round from the waist as the club goes up,
and untwisting it as the club comes down. That
is why I say that, having taken up your stance
you must not move out of the space which you
occupy as you address the ball. It is purely a
matter of winding yourself up with the arms, and
unwinding yourself with the arms. Or perhaps
I might have said with the club, because it is
important to remember that the club-head should
always lead. The whole movement is a turn of
the body on its own axis. Imagine that, at the
waist and neck, you have rings of wheels on
which your body will twist round so that the
club and the arms can turn it without causing
the head to move or the nether limbs to shift
more than is necessary to preserve a balance. Let
us consider the arms, which, with the club leading them, so to speak, promote this process of
winding and unwinding. If I may so explain it,
each half of the golf swing—the upward and
the downward—consists of two distinct movements
which fit so perfectly into one another as to produce a rhythmic whole. Most of my readers
have doubtless seen that mechanical kind of doll
which raises its hand automatically. With the
first jerk, the arm goes half-way up; with the
second, it touches the head as though saluting.
If that arm worked at the side instead of at the
front, it would afford a fair notion of the action
for the golf swing. It would give, at any rate,

the germ of the idea. I do not mean to suggest that the golfer should behave as though he had to wait for a button to be pressed before he could lift his arm beyond a certain point. There must be no spasmodic jerking. But the fact remains that the upward swing is made by two movements, one dovetailing so nicely into the other as to render the complete operation smooth and continuous. The first movement raises the club until its head is pointing upwards, the right hip screwing round the while. The second movement makes the elbows bend and lets the shaft fall into position behind the player's head. As the shaft thus drops, the palms of the hands open a little and the grip is relaxed, save for that exercised by the thumbs and forefingers, which are the grippers-in-chief. To demonstrate the latter fact, I have often held a club solely with the thumbs and forefingers, all the other fingers being off the shaft, and made satisfactory shots. Those other fingers, however, are very useful for guiding the club at all parts of the swing, and I do not mean to suggest that they should ever be off the shaft. They should simply loosen their hold a trifle as the elbows bend; they will regain of their own accord a firmer grip as the club comes down. At the top of the swing the shaft should be so close to the player's head, without touching it, as to render impossible the wearing of a hat with a brim—or, at any rate, a hard brim. Sometimes one sees ladies golfing in large straw hats. They simply cannot be swinging properly. or they would knock their hats every time.

It is surprising how many golfers omit to perform the second movement in the swing. They raise the club stiffly and seem to consider that the highest point in the air which they can reach must represent the top of the swing, and

that there is consequently no need to go back
any farther. This half-swing is not nearly so
great a handicap with the rubber-cored ball as it
was with the gutty, but it is an incomplete way of
playing golf. The person who adopts such a
style is, I suppose, impressed with the necessity
of " sweeping " the ball away instead of hitting
it. He has been enjoined so often to " sweep "
it off the tee or the fairway that he thinks he
cannot do better than describe a sort of semicircle
with the club-head. The idea of the sweeping
action is very well, but the golf swing is not a
sweep pure and simple. It is partly a hit. And
the natural method of getting into position for
hitting with a stick or any other instrument is
to have it behind your head so that you can lash
round strongly with it. Well, you want to lash
round at the golf ball, but it is essential to
exercise restraint as the club begins to come
down. It must be travelling at its fastest pace at
the moment of impact. To make it do so is the
art of the swing. It is the knack that introduces
the sweeping action with power behind it.

Up to the present I have not attempted to
describe *seriatim* the actions which produce the
perfect swing. I have endeavoured to emphasize
a fact which is unknown to or unhonoured by
thousands of players, to their frequent discomfiture—namely, that the operation consists of
twisting the body corkscrew-like by the aid of the
club and arms; not of lurching away from the
ball, and then making a hefty lunge at it. That
point having been appreciated, let us now consider
the operation in detail. The stance is comfortable; the toes are pointing outwards; the ball is
distinctly nearer the left heel than the right, and
the right foot is a few inches in front of the left
—or, at any rate, not behind it—so as to facilitate

the finish.   Begin by taking the club-head back
almost parallel with the ground for a few inches.
It must, however, rise a little.   At the same time
start to turn the left wrist inwards towards the
body and to screw the right hip round towards
the back.   If the head be rigid, the top of the
left leg has to turn and move outwards a trifle
in response to the pressure from the right hip.
It cannot do anything else since something has
to give way.   As a natural result, that left knee
bends.   The right leg should be almost stiff.
There is the inauguration of the winding-up
process, which has merely to be continued to
produce the desired effect.   The body must be
screwed up as far as it will go, and to prevent
it from trying to escape the ordeal by a slacken-
ing of the legs, it is necessary to see that the
left heel, although it rises, does not turn out of
position to any appreciable extent.   The pivoting
on the left foot must be done on the inside of
that foot, from the big joint to the end of the
big toe.   Here, then, we have the body wound
up—the left wrist, the right hip, the top of the
left leg, and so down to the ankle, all screwing in
sympathy and producing a spiral-like attitude.
To make certain of none of the effect of this
twisting slipping away, it is important to
remember to press firmly on the ball of the left
foot and not to shift the heel sideways.   The
strain will be felt a little; it should be.   Having
wound up the body as tightly as possible "trussed
like a fowl," as I once heard the position described,
although even a prepared fowl is not twisted so
much), no part of the mechanism must be allowed
to slip.   As it was screwed so must it be
unscrewed.

If you have gone up properly, you ought to
experience little difficulty in coming down cor-

Stance

THE DRIVE OR BRASSIE SHOT

Top of the swing. The head has remained practically still save for a slight turn. It has not swayed. The right leg has stiffened with the screwing of the hips, and the left knee has bent inwards

Finish. All the body movement has been done from the hips, and even at the end of the follow-through, the head has moved only very slightly towards the hole

rectly. I do not say—as some people do—that
you are sure to come down correctly, because
you may make the grievous mistake of throwing
out your arms. There is one admirable means of
preventing such a sure producer of disaster. It
is to aim at an imaginary something to the right
of the player and about a foot behind the line
in which he is standing. In teaching the game,
I often take up a position such as that indicated
for the "something" and say to the pupil,
"Now try to hit me as you bring the club down.
I'll see that you don't, but try to." The idea
can be practised by placing any object at a point
towards which the club should go at the beginning of the downward swing. The only road to
a straight shot is to send the club well out to
the right and a little behind the body at the
beginning of the downward swing. Then it will
come round with a "Swish," gathering pace all
the while, and the ball will go as straight as an
arrow—well, as far as you can send it.

Arnaud Massy has a curious custom which
never fails to put his club on the right track at
the start of the downward swing. It has aroused
a lot of comment from time to time. I have
seen it described as Massy's "pig-tail," Massy's
"twiddley-bit" and whatnot, and a great deal
of wonderment has been expressed as to why
the Frenchman does it and the possible effects of
it. What happens is, that, at the top of the
swing, Massy makes a strange little flourish, a
circling in the air, with the head of his club.
Whereas most men, having gone up, promptly
start to come down again, Massy waits to perform
this "twiddley-bit." It would be a fine thing
for any of us if we possessed the same habit.
By giving the club-head that little turn at the
top, he pushes it out behind him so that it is

almost certain to come down right. It is practically impossible for him to throw his arms forward since they have been urged into the proper track by that flourish which makes the club-head circle away from him. For the average golfer, however, it is sufficient to remember to aim slightly behind at the beginning of the downward swing. There should be no movement at all, except of the arms, until the club is halfway down. It must be first recovered from behind the head while the loosened fingers are coming back on to the shaft. Then, when it is well out to the right a point or two behind the player, and just beginning to gain impetus, the whole body unwinds, round comes the club, and the stroke is a fine one. A good swing is a certain means of hitting the ball. In order to convince pupils of that fact, I have often closed my eyes tightly and driven without looking at the ball after having taken up the stance and made the address. The proper swing cannot fail.

Yet it is certain that the majority of golfers sow the seeds of a foozle in the first movement. As the average player takes the club back, he moves his body in the same direction and throws all the weight on to his right leg. At once everything starts to go wrong. It is a natural inclination, but it is easy to overcome if you determine that, rather than go the same way as the club, you will go the opposite way. The proper thing, however, is not to disturb the balance at all. A common failing which is wrapped, so to speak, in the one just described, is that the player does not fight against the left shoulder. He perhaps starts the upward swing well enough, but then he sees the left shoulder coming under his chin—which is just where it ought to be at the top of the swing. But it

COMING DOWN

The wrong downward swing. The body has turned too soon and the club has therefore been pushed forward

As the club should come down, i.e., behind the player

takes him by surprise and seems to alarm him.
He dodges away from it, and the result is a
wrong back swing. Rather let him move, if
move he must, in the opposite direction.

I have said nothing about the follow-through
because it is the result of the method; it is not
the method itself. If the swing has been properly
executed the follow-through will be all right with
the body twisting round so much as to be facing
the hole. The head will be over the right shoulder
leaning towards the spot from which the ball has
been dispatched. It will go forward with the
body a few inches as a result of the momentum
which it has obtained during the downward swing.
That will be its first movement. If the head
be erect it must have been moved too soon,
producing, in most cases, a top

"Slow back" is an excellent rule for the
novice, and even for the advanced golfer. But
by " slow back " I do not mean taking the implement back at snail's pace. Very often the maxim
is dinned into the ears of the beginner with such
assiduity that he worries himself almost to death
in his endeavours to make the upward swing as
slow as possible. That is as bad as too rapid a
movement. There is a happy medium. As proficiency encourages confidence, the back swing
is apt to become faster and faster, but there is
no advantage in that development, because there
is nothing to hit at the top. Sometimes one
sees a player take the club up at lightning pace,
with the result that it not only drops behind
his head, but reaches very nearly down to his
heels. Pursuing that plan, the golfer can depend
upon suffering fairly often from the effects of
overswinging. He has to loosen his grip entirely
and hurl himself forward to hit the ball.

Now we have seen the operation as it should

be—the inward turn of the left wrist, the screwing round of the right hip, the pivoting on the inside of the left foot, the bend of the elbows that causes the grip to temporarily relax (save for the thumbs and forefingers) and the shaft to drop behind the head, the aiming at an imaginary object to the right about a foot behind the player, and then the natural sweep round of the club which strikes the ball smoothly, yet with all the power of a hit, and finds the weight equally distributed, as it was during the address. If, instead of winding up the body, you merely move it to one side, you shift the weight so far away that you cannot often get it back in time for the impact.

When the ball is "cupped," and the player still desires to use a brassie through the green, it is useless to endeavour to nip right into a small indentation in the ground and at the same time get well under the ball. The disposition to attempt it may be strong, because it seems that one ought to make sure of lifting the ball out of the depression, but it will come out all right if the player aim an inch or two behind the object. What he needs to do is to make the club cut through the edge of the cup—that is to say, through the top of the turf which forms the cup. That will enable him to get at the ball. Consequently, whether he aims one inch or two inches behind the ball depends upon the extent to which it is ensconced in the abominable hollow. With the rubber-core, however, there is seldom real necessity to take a brassie in a cuppy lie. An iron club will usually obtain the required distance. That is one more phase of the simplifying of golf.

These are seven golden rules of the golf drive : —

FAULTY MOVEMENTS

A wrong back swing and perhaps the most common of faults. The body is swaying away from the ball. The left arm is too high and the position of the left wrist is very bad. It will be observed that the in-dicator has signalled the mistake

A wrong position at the top of the swing. The head and body have straightened, making it very difficult for them to resume the same position as during the address. The left knee is not sufficiently bent, and the left shoulder when coming round has pushed the head out of position

A wrong finish. The body is leaning away from the ball and towards the pole at the back. The head has been lifted too soon, and the result will usually be either a top or a slice

1. Keep the head steady and do not let the left heel turn outwards—then the body can only wind up when the arms go back.

2. Grip firmest with the thumbs and forefingers —they are not so well adapted as the other fingers to the purposes of taking a strong hold, and they are the most important of all for the purpose of the golf grip.

3. Let the club-head lead, the left wrist turning inwards, the arms following the club-head, and the right hip screwing next.

4. Don't throw the arms forward as you start to come down as though you were mowing grass. Rather throw them back, and let them come round in their own way from that point.

5. Let the movement of the right shoulder be steady and rhythmic; it should have nothing in the nature of a sudden drop or jerk.

6. Don't be afraid to hit hard; if you are swinging correctly, hard hitting is not " pressing."

7. Keep your head still until the club has struck the ball.

CHAPTER VI

CLEEK AND IRON SHOTS

WHEN the iron-headed clubs come up for discussion, the golfer's first thoughts turn instinctively to the cleek. It is not an easy implement with which to obtain good results, but once the player feels confident of his ability to use it properly, he is equipped with a tool which is invaluable. It can be employed with profit for many kinds of strokes. In these days of the rubber-cored ball, it is possible to get very nearly as far with the club in question as with a driver or brassie, so that to the player who hesitates to attempt a full wooden-club shot when the lie is indifferent, the cleek presents itself in the nature of a providential saver of the situation. Far better, too, is it to play a half shot with the cleek than a full swipe with the iron. Here, then, we have an agent capable of doing much good. Now as to the best way to become on friendly terms with it. The best way is, I think, to obtain an introduction to it through the medium of the iron.

Let us assume that the aspirant to success is master of the swing. That is essential. He is making drives and brassie shots of eminently respectable extent and direction. On the hard

78

ground, he may be even merging himself in the general conspiracy to spoil the courses by driving unreasonably far. He is swinging properly; therefore he can turn with self-reliance to the task of learning the peculiarities of the cleek and iron. Those peculiarities are few.

I said earlier in this book that the easiest shots in golf were those made from the tee with a brassie and from the fairway with an ordinary iron. The latter club is a general favourite. Its loft is not stinted like that of the cleek, nor accentuated like that of the mashie. It is a rational, attractive sort of loft; just the kind required to pick a ball up cleanly from the turf and send it hurling through space. Without a doubt, the iron, in addition to being a useful implement, enjoys immense popularity, and is quick to win the confidence of its owner. It might almost be described as the pet of the bag. Nor is it often a spoilt child. One seldom hears a golfer complaining that this particular club is not what it ought to be. From time to time he may fancy another iron, and buy it, but only because he is devoted to irons just as some people have a passion for foreign stamps. It is not because he feels that his first friend has played him false.

This widespread sentiment is alone a sufficiently good reason for recommending an early course of study with the iron to the beginner or the person who is endeavouring to rise superior to long-standing mediocrity. He can intersperse such practice with that which he is obtaining with the wooden clubs. Just as he will be able to use the driver if he become competent with the brassie on the teeing ground, so will he be able to do good work with the cleek if he can make satisfactory shots with his iron. In each case, it is a matter of beginning with the easier article and so lessening the difficulties of the harder one. The manner of swinging by turning from the waist and pivoting on the left big toe without turning the heel outwards is—or should be—precisely the same for all four of the clubs. By all means grip a little tighter with the cleek or iron than with the driver or brassie, but the chief differences in the methods of executing iron and wooden-club shots are matters of stance and length of back swing. The slightly strengthened hold is desirable lest the implement turn in the hands at the moment of impact, a disaster which is apt to occur through the contact with the ground; but I cannot support the advice which I have seen given in some treatises that the grip with iron implements should be so tight as to make the blood run out of the knuckles. The person who clutches the handle with that degree of grim desperation is likely to get himself into a state of uncomfortable tautness. Just grip with such firmness, more especially with the thumbs and forefingers, as to prevent the club from twisting in the hands. If you remember the thumbs and forefingers, the other fingers will generally supply of their own accord the desired amount of pressure. Or, at least, they will very soon come to know what is required of them.

Whatever shot the player may be practising, he should adopt the simple means which I have already mentioned of training his head to keep still; for the head that does not move during the swing belongs to the man who is going to succeed on the links. I may be accused of labouring this point to excess, but I am convinced that, for the person whose ability is now moderate, the rigid head until the beginning of the follow-through is a necessity the importance of which cannot be overrated. A first-class player knows whenever he moves his head, and realizes that he must bring his club down differently from the way in which it went up. Moreover, his knowledge of the game is such that he can recover during the swing. I do not for a moment urge that a champion never moves his head, but I do say that he very seldom shifts it in anything like the same degree as a bad player. For the latter to change the position to the extent of twelve or fifteen inches during the back swing is one of the commonest sights in the world. It is a mortal offence to the art of golf, and the prime determination of the indifferent performer should be to repress it. When the first-class player moves his head, the change is, as a rule, so small as to be almost imperceptible. Yet he personally is aware of it, and his errant head retrieves the situation by thinking to work the club back into the proper position during the downward swing. It is too much to expect the average golfer to recover in this way; therefore it is a more important matter for him to keep his head still than it is in the case of the accomplished player.

Up to the present, we have observed no great dissimilarity between wooden-club shots and iron-club shots. The first difference is in the matter of the stance. As a rule, the cleek is two or three inches shorter than the driver or brassie, while the iron is a little shorter than the cleek. These variations are desirable, and the point to remember is that the shorter the shaft the nearer to the ball the player must stand. Sometimes one sees a person standing as far off for an iron shot as he would do for a drive, and reaching the ball by stooping down to it. It is an impossible way of executing the required stroke. The toe of the club is cocked up in the air, the body is cramped, and an easy swing is out of the question. The

F

proper method, as it is certainly the simplest, is to get a trifle nearer for every inch that the shaft is shorter than that of the wooden clubs. You simply close in on the ball, so to speak, in order to be able to reach it without undue bending. For the cleek the feet are drawn just a little closer together than for the driver or brassie; the ball is distinctly nearer to the player. For the iron, the stance is closer still. The arms should have just sufficient room to swing through freely as the club descends to perform its work. They should not be allowed to touch the body; but in no circumstances should they be stretched forward, because it is necessary to preserve a perfect balance. However, if you remember not to stoop more for these shots than for drives, you will naturally take up a position the proper distance from the ball, and then the arms will not be induced to do wayward tricks.

The nearer the player is to the ball, the more upright will be the swing. That is inevitable. For the iron clubs, the swing ought to be more upright than for the driver or brassie. It should be a more compact action altogether. Generally speaking, the position of the left foot should alter less than that of the right—taking the drive as the basis for the stance. For a cleek or iron shot, as for a stroke with a wooden club, the ball should be on a line with a point a few inches inside the left heel; but the right foot should be brought nearer to the left so as to allow for the introduction of that element of uprightness into the swing. The left may be an inch or so forward, but the distance between the two feet should be lessened, mainly as a result of the right's advance. When the player takes the iron he should turn his body slightly towards the hole. That change will place the right foot even closer to the ball than the left.

THE CLEEK SHOT

Stance. The player is distinctly nearer to the ball than for the drives

Top of the swing

Finish

The learner likes to hit hard, and he should begin his course of education with the iron by making full shots. He should aim from half an inch to an inch behind the ball. He will find the shots comparatively easy and—when he executes them properly—soul-satisfying. Except for that degree of uprightness, which is enforced by the fact of the feet being closer together, the swing should be the same as for the wooden clubs. It should consist of just the same old operation of winding up the body from the hips as the arms go back, pivoting on the inside of the left foot from the big joint to the big toe, and unwinding the body as the arms return. If the feet are too far apart, it is impossible to pivot properly. When the left heel turns outwards, it is certain that the player is lurching his body.

Do not forget to aim at a spot half an inch or even an inch behind the ball. This applies to the cleek as well as to the iron. The place on which you need to fix the eye is the small gap between the ball and the club when the latter is grounded preparatory to the making of the shot. If you recollect at this moment of the completion of the address to direct the vision at that little gap, you will see the side of the ball, which is the part you want to hit. It is desirable to remember not to have the arms tucked right into the body. This is a fairly common fault; the player, having drawn nearer to the ball, seems to be possessed by an impulse to keep his arms so close in that they touch his body. They should be clear.

The distance of the shot should be governed by the length of the back swing. It is a great thing to always hit the ball unfalteringly. When only a half shot is needed, it is bad to take the club right back, and then try to check it at the moment of impact so as to prevent the ball going too far.

One often sees this done, and the result is nearly always a foozle. Judgment in the execution of approaches depends not upon deciding how hard to strike the ball. The real judgment consists of knowing just how far to take the club back. Every player must find out for himself how far he can hit with various lengths of back swings; the only warning I offer is against the fairly common habit of paying no attention at all to the back swing, and trying to apply a certain strength just as the club meets the ball. I fear nobody could do that with much success. When a man goes back a long way for a half shot, he realizes at the critical moment that he must slow up a little or he will overshoot the mark. Then it is that the whole swing flounders, and the shot with it.

Don't stoop unduly when using the cleek or iron. Many people do this, more particularly when they take up a stance for the iron. If you desire to get up to the top of the swing, and you start in a squatting attitude, you will simply bob up and down. And absolute steadiness of stance is even more important with iron clubs than with the driver. An inclination to lift the body, which is born of a crouching posture during the address, is fatal.

As alternative clubs to the cleek, there are the driving-mashie and the spoon. Each has its virtues. A passing fancy sometimes makes the driving-mashie a highly effective instrument, while the spoon is the favourite implement of many golfers. By reason of its loft, it is easier to use than the cleek, but the latter, when mastered, is by far the more likely, I think, to place the ball near the hole. It is the more complaisant in the matter of guiding the ball. Still, much splendid work can be done with the spoon, as George Duncan and Sandy Herd have shown us, and I

THE IRON SHOT

Stance. The player has drawn nearer to the ball than for the cleek, and the body is turned a little more towards the hole

Top of the swing

Finish

would merely advise golfers who conceive a liking for the club not to allow it to turn the cleek out of the bag. They doubtless wish to advance; and certain shots can be made with the cleek which are practically outside the range of possibility with the spoon. There is, for instance, the " push," which can be described later. If the driving-mashie or spoon exercise a sudden fascination over the player, by all means let him succumb, and see how he likes it. The stance for either of these alternative weapons is the same as for the cleek, which, in due course, he will doubtless reinstate as a friend capable of helping him in times of need.

Of late there has come into vogue a club called the wooden cleek, which is helpful to the bad golfer because it has a deeper and broader face than the iron-headed cleek. The loft is the same as in the case of the latter instrument, but the big face of the wooden cleek inspires confidence. There is such a large area with which to hit the ball that the doubter becomes trusting; he feels that some part of the club, anyhow, will realize his hopes. It requires a good lie; but if the player is convinced that it is easier to use than the ordinary cleek, let him use it. It is surprising what a conviction of this kind will do. A case came under my notice not long ago. It was that of a man who vowed that he could always hit a good shot with his iron, but that he was sure to miss the ball with his cleek. One day he decided to take a risk. " Give me the cleek," he said to the caddie. " I'll chance it." Sure enough, he missed the globe three times. " It's no use," he declared, " I must have the iron." The caddie rummaged in the bag, and then glanced at his employer. " Why," he said, " you've got it." Truly enough, the player thought he had been

using the cleek, and had simply frightened himself into failure. Directly he realized that he had
the iron in his hands, he hit the ball. This story
may sound exaggerated, but it is the truth; nothing but the truth.

CHAPTER VII

MASHIE SHOTS

WE make a bow to the mashie. Let it be a friendly yet respectful salutation, born of a determination to render the introduction mutually pleasant. For the production of its best points, the mashie needs a special disposition of the player's mental and physical forces. It requires management of a kind which is different in several important details from that bestowed upon the driver, brassie, cleek, iron, and kindred instruments. It is a club that demands the utmost precision in our handling of it; for it is exceedingly susceptible to the slightest departure from the correct methods. That is why it seems to be about the most fickle of golfing tools; one day the best helpmate in the world, and on another occasion, the very deuce. The reason is that it is docile and obliging in the highest degree when it receives proper treatment, but that any small error of omission or commission transforms it into a veritable demon of refractoriness. True it is that the rubber-cored ball has helped to mitigate the horrors which this severely dignified implement would gladly heap upon the head of the person who used it in a way of which it disapproved. We have all seen players make bad mashie shots and still reach the green. That hardly ever happened when the gutta-percha ball was in vogue, and even now the percentage of poor shots that enjoy happy endings is not nearly so large in the case of the mashie as it is where other clubs are concerned. On hard ground, a miss with the driver, brassie, cleek, or iron frequently entails no serious consequences; but a foozle with the mashie does not often go unpenalized. A top, for instance, will usually send the ball into a bunker, or scuttling over the green. There is cause for complaint in the fact that a good mashie shot is occasionally punished, but this is generally due to abnormal condition of the turf or faults in the slopes of the ground. Taken all round, there is no more influential club than the mashie, and to the golfer who experiences difficulty with it, I would recommend a period of practice with it almost every day. Such assiduity will be repaid.

The feature of the mashie shot, the trait that distinguishes it from every other stroke which we have so far studied, is explainable in these words: It depends primarily upon the movements of the knees. Hitherto we have been winding up and unwinding our bodies from the neck to the very toes. Now that we have the mashie in hand, the process of winding and unwinding will be renewed; but it must not be allowed to have serious influence below the knees. The less it causes the feet to shift the better. We want to be very steady on our feet—almost as steady as if they were stuck to the ground. As they do not happen to be so fastened (except, perhaps, during the winter months on those courses of tenacious clay) we shall move them a trifle; but, if possible, we shall not lift either heel off the ground. The outstanding fault of most bad

players in this branch of the game is that they
do not use their knees sufficiently. Their methods
are of many varieties, and sometimes almost indescribable; but in the abstract, their fatal error
is that they regard a mashie as being of the
same breed as an iron. It is of a different nature,
and except in the case of a first-class golfer,
who has acquired by lifelong study a mastery
over the club which enables him to take liberties
with it, the mashie simply will not tolerate such
discourtesy.

For the ordinary golfer, I would seldom recommend more than a three-quarter swing with
this particular (very particular) club, and there
should be no pirouetting. I do not mean to
suggest that wild exuberance on the feet is tolerable with the clubs of longer range, but we
know that when we take those implements, we
want to turn freely and pivot on the inside of
the left foot, from the big joint to the end of
the big toe. In the ordinary way, we do not
foot-pivot with the mashie. The club objects to
it. Our first necessity is to obtain stability of
stance, because we need to be exact in the way
in which we strike the ball, and even a small
measure of the foot freedom in which we have
previously revelled may cause us to apply
the wrong strength or direction to the shot.

Sometimes it is necessary to make a neck-or-
nothing swipe with a mashie, but those occasions
are rare. Indeed, they are presented only when
it is a matter of carrying some high trees, or
other lofty obstacles. Placed in such a situation,
the golfer may reasonably feel constrained to
take a full swing, and then he will have to stand
in much the same way as for the iron, and pivot
on the left foot in the manner previously described.
In most cases, however, he will not need more

than a half or three-quarter swing with a mashie
because, in normal circumstances, he will be
well advised to use the club only when he finds
himself within, say, one hundred yards of the
hole.

Let us first consider the stance.   The player
should be nearer to the ball than for the iron,
with his body turned well towards the hole.   The
left foot should be pointing outwards; the ball
should be almost opposite the left heel.   The
position of the right foot is of even greater
importance.   Nearly all the data that can be
brought to bear on the subject supports the con-
tention that it is best to play mashie shots off
the right leg.   The right foot should be well in
front of the left, and nearer to the ball than it
has been for any other shot which we have thus
far discussed.   It should occupy a line which, if
extended, would be parallel with the sole of the
club.   In this, as in other strokes, it is necessary
to ground the implement so that the striking
surface is at right angles to the direction in
which we are hoping to make our way.   It is
clear that if the golfer place his right foot in a
line parallel with the sole of his mashie, and
have his left foot pointing outwards, with the
ball opposite the heel of that foot, he must turn
his body towards the green.   He cannot well
do anything else.   He will turn it to just the
proper extent if he remembers to have the sole
of the club and the right foot absolutely square
to the line of play.   Standing thus, with the feet
sufficiently close together to permit of a comfortable bending of the knees, he will be in the
correct position for the most common form of
mashie shot, which is the pitch-and-run.   The
stance is a matter of great consequence, and it
should be closely studied.

Stance. The right knee is appreciably bent, and most of the weight is on the right leg

THE ORDINARY MASHIE SHOT

Top of the swing. The right knee has stiffened. The left knee has bent, and is supporting the greater part of the weight. The hips have turned slightly, but most of the pivoting has been done at the knees

Now as to the method of winding up and unwinding the body; that is to say, the method of making the swing. As I have already said, the knees are all-important. There should be no rigidity about any part of the body except the head and feet. The head must be still; and the feet must be planted firmly on the ground. For the rest, the posture should be one of moderate relaxation, with a distinct element of slackness at the knees. The pivoting, so to speak, has to be done at the knees, which must be in such a position at the start that they can control the twisting of the body without allowing such twisting to be communicated to the feet. In short, the player practically screws himself into position with his knees, and unscrews himself with his knees—although he must not forget to so " time " the movements of his arms and hips that they work in perfect unison with the lower joints. Knees, hips, and arms should act in concert; the proper swing for the mashie will then result.

As the player stands addressing the ball with a firm grip of the club, especially in regard to the thumbs and forefingers, let the weight of the body be supported by the right leg. To get comfortably into that position, it will be necessary to bend the right knee. As the club is taken back, the body screwing round at the hips rather less freely than in the case of longer shots, the right leg naturally stiffens. In fact, the knee of that leg really governs the stroke. Directly it is rigid, the screwing should stop. The backward swing is complete. The left knee will have bent slightly, as shown in the photograph of the mashie shot at the top of the swing.

It cannot have avoided doing so if you have remembered not to lift the foot from the ground

The safest advice is that the player should not raise either heel from the ground when executing anything less than a full mashie shot. And the latter, as I have already said, is merely a stroke for an exceptional occasion. For the three-quarter, half, or shorter swing—that is to say, for the normal mashie shot—the left foot should be flat on the turf as the left knee bends outwards. It is easily possible to obtain a three-quarter swing without moving that foot one iota. The downward swing, which amounts to unwinding the body by returning the right knee to the bent position, ought to be satisfactory so long as the player resists these three common failings: —Dropping the right shoulder with a jerk; bending the right wrist at the moment of impact in a sudden effort to push the club under the ball; and looking up too quickly. These are golfing sins in any kind of shot; but the temptation to commit them is never stronger than when the mashie is being used. The right shoulder should come round with rhythmic steadiness, and it will usually do so if the executant sternly repress the inclination to bend his right wrist as he comes to the ball—the result of a flash of fear that he may not, after all, get the face of the club under the object. The club will go under the ball all right if the swing be proper. The player should aim, as with the iron, about half an inch behind the ball; the loft of the mashie will then do what so many persons try to accomplish with their right wrists. I am certain that forty of every fifty bad golfers owe their weakness with the mashie to this obsession in the matter of trying to shovel the ball into the air. They endeavour to carry it, so to speak, on the face of the club. That is impossible. What usually happens is that they strike the ground about three inches behind

For a stroke of, say 80 yards. The position is one of comfort, obviously nothing like hard work has been associated with it, and the weight is equally divided

FINISH OF THE ORDINARY MASHIE SHOT

For a shot of less distance

the ball, and a fearful foozle results. If they could summon the determination to hit their mashie shots with the same freedom from anxiety to scoop the ball as they enjoy when they are driving, they would improve rapidly. The club will produce the loft; the player need not bother about it. A good golfer when using the mashie thumps the ball. He never scoops it. That is the difference between the right way and the wrong way.

The desire to look up quickly is a natural one. When we are playing an approach of this kind, the spot which we are trying to reach is near and well defined. It is the space within a few yards of the flag. Consequently, there is anxiety to see immediately whether the ball is there. It will never be there unless we look at it long enough to strike it accurately. The head must be kept still with heroic determination until the follow-through is under way. The action of the right foot is purely a matter of the finish, when the ball has been despatched on its journey; but the player will be assisted to preserve the correct balance for the whole stroke if he determine to have that right foot fixed to the ground even at the end of the shot. He can move it to such an extent that he turns to the inside of it at the finish of the follow-through but he should be chary of lifting either heel off the turf at any point of the swing. It is dangerous to give such freedom to the feet, because it is apt to undermine that perfect stability of stance which is so necessary.

Here, then, we have the formula for the ordinary pitch-and-run stroke with the mashie—a formula which has the approval in practice of all the good players I have seen, and the principles of which apply from the three-quarter swing down to the little chip. There is another shot of a more complicated character. It is the mashie stroke played with cut. It is one of the shots that have helped to raise golf to the standard of an art. Unfortunately, it does not now produce with such certainty the effects which it invariably gave in those days of the gutty. It was possible in those times to pitch the ball right up to the hole with the assurance that, if the cut had been properly applied, there would not be a yard of run at the finish of the carry. The distance had to be accurately estimated; and the ability to impart the spin had to be cultivated. Knowledge systematized and practised in this way would give the desired result with unfailing regularity. Nowadays one cannot always be sure what the ball will do. It is necessary to allow for a certain amount of run, and my own personal experience is that the player is apt to change his mind during the swing as to the spot at which he shall make the ball alight. He does not know how far it will skid, even though it be influenced by all the cut imaginable. It is a great pity that this element of uncertainty has been introduced into a really beautiful shot. Another misfortune is that many of the younger golfers of undoubted skill are so imbued with the spirit that makes them play for the pull that they never try to master this shot, which is nearly all carry. They do nothing but pitch and run.

Still, if the mashie shot with cut has been discouraged by the bouncing properties of the rubber-core, it remains a valuable stroke, and often the only one that can be attempted with any hope of laying the ball close to the hole. We may feel almost distracted when we reflect that, in any case, it is sure to run some distance, we

Stance

THE MASHIE SHOT WITH CUT

Beginning of the upward swing. The club has gone outwards instead of behind

Top of the swing. The left knee has bent forward considerably. This is in response to the desire to get the head into proper position after the slight sway enforced by the body following the club at the start of the swing

know not what; but we must try it when we realize that the ordinary shot will of a certainty run too far. The stance is naturally a matter of great importance.

There should be, as previously, a distinct bend at the knees. The right foot should be advanced two or three inches nearer to the ball. The left foot should be drawn back a little, making the toe point more towards the hole than ever. The ball should be just about opposite the middle of the left foot. It can be readily perceived that the effect of this stance will be to turn the whole body more in the direction of the hole than for the plain mashie stroke. That is as it should be.

Now what we want to do is to draw the face of the club quickly and cleanly across the ball at the instant of impact. At the critical moment, the implement must be travelling across the line of flight, from right to left, so that directly it touches the ball the latter begins to spin. Clearly, then, we shall not swing as in ordinary circumstances. This cut shot is one of the few strokes in golf in which the head and body must—and should—sway a trifle as the club goes up.

Instead of keeping the arms close to the body, the player should push them away from him during the backward swing. He should push them away to such an extent that, as the right knee stiffens, the weight is thrown on to that leg instead of on to the left. There will be no twisting at the hips. The body will simply follow the club back. It is the necessity of this slight swaying movement that renders the shot so difficult of perfect accomplishment. Do not strain to take the mashie up too far (the cut shot is generally a fairly short one); then there will be little danger of overswaying. The club will come down in the same track as that which it occupied when ascending. At the moment of impact the arms should straighten, and the wrists should tighten. From the nature of the upward swing, the club is necessarily coming down across the ball, but everything should be done to accentuate that effect. Do not be afraid to make a distinct attempt to draw the mashie sharply and cleanly across the ball at the instant when the two come into contact. It is a shot for a skilful golfer because, to make the most of it, the object must be struck with the utmost accuracy. For that reason, it is advisable to hold the club at the lower part of the grip, the better to keep the head of the implement under complete control. The place to play for is a spot a yard or so to the left of the pin since the ball, if cut in the proper way, will naturally screw to the right on reaching the ground.

Nowadays, a great number of people like to play their approaches with niblicks. Being much more lofted than the mashie, the niblick is well suited to the purpose. It imbues the golfer with a deal of confidence, inasmuch as he feels that the ball will not run far from such a club. And confidence is an asset. For the indifferent golfer, however, I cannot help thinking that the niblick is considerably harder to use than the mashie. The former club usually has a very sharp edge, and unless the ball be hit with great precision, that edge is apt to stick into the ground and spoil the shot as well as the turf. Nowadays tools called mashie-niblicks are popular. A warning that I would offer to the player who fancies a niblick for approaching is that he should not use it on an important occasion unless he is thoroughly intimate with it. To know the driving power of the club is essential.

Finish for a stroke of medium length **THE MASHIE SHOT WITH CUT** *Finish for a longer shot (say 50 to 70 yards)*

That power varies amazingly in different niblicks, and unless you are aware from constant
use how far the ball will go off the implement,
it is better to employ an ordinary mashie. And
once you have come to understand the strength
of your niblick in approach shots, do not change
it because it fails you once or twice—unless, of
course, it has an obvious fault. It will take you
a long while to learn the peculiarities of another.
To know your niblick—if you employ it for that
department of the game which we are discussing
—is a matter of supreme importance. In
bunkers, you often have to use it whether you
are on good terms with it or not.

Personally, I have come to like the club very
well for approaching. It was with a niblick that
I played the best shot of my life. The occasion
was a tournament at Northwood a few years
ago. At the eighteenth hole, I sliced my second
shot. The ball lay within about four feet of the
club-house, which was now between me and
the hole. As you can imagine, it was a pretty
big stymie, and for a while I hardly knew how
to tackle it except by playing out to the left.
At last I decided to try and carry the building,
and reach the green. The people on the veranda
looked rather surprised when I asked them to
stand aside in case I should strike them. The
veranda was protected by wire netting, but I knew
that I should have to hit the ball hard to make
it rise almost straight into the air until it reached
the top of the club-house, and put enough spin
on it to cause it to carry forward thirty yards
to the green. It is not difficult to get a ball
to rise almost perpendicularly, but to make it
start to move forward when it is thirty or forty
feet from the ground is a different matter, and
I was afraid that, if the shot failed, I might

G

send the ball through the netting and hit somebody.

So, smilingly, they moved aside. I used a niblick for the shot. The ball flew up, moving forward no more than a yard until it was about thirty feet in the air; then it went on, carried the club-house, and stopped a yard from the hole. And then I missed the putt. That was a wretched finish; but the shot from directly behind the building was the best I ever played, and I am frankly and boyishly proud of it.

Occasions when the running-up approach offers the simplest means of reaching the vicinity of the hole are becoming more and more numerous. There are not so many cross-bunkers as there used to be, and, in their absence, it is sometimes safest to keep such a lively article as the rubber-cored ball close to the ground all the way. For this stroke it is desirable to stand more forward than for the ordinary mashie shot; the hands should be in front of the ball. This will tend to keep the ball low. If the shot is being played with an iron or mashie so as to produce a slight loft at the start in order to skim over rough ground and finish with a run, it is necessary to impart a pull to the ball. The pull will make it run; without that influence, the ball might collide with a wormcast, or some other obstacle, and stop almost immediately. With the pull, it will go forward in spite of its contact with such an unnecessary nuisance. The thing is easily done. It is a matter of striking the back of the ball quite cleanly, and turning the right hand over at the moment of impact. That turning over of the right hand (the action of locking a door with a key, as it has been aptly described by Mr. J. L. Low) is the essence of the pull. It is important, however, not to make the action

THE RUNNING-UP SHOT

Stance. The hands are in front of the ball, which is opposite the right heel

Top of the swing. As will be seen by a glance at the pole at the back the body has moved considerably forward towards the hole from the stance. The club is going to describe practically a semicircle

THE RUNNING-UP SHOT

*Finish. The right hand has turned half over, as will be seen by comparing this picture with that
of the finish for the ordinary mashie shot. The body is almost erect, with the head leaning towards
where the ball has been, but this position must not be assumed until the ball has been struck*

too emphatic. Perhaps it would be better to suggest a half-turn of the key in the lock in order to produce the right effect on the golf course. The distance which you take the club back must be governed, as in other cases, by the length of shot required, but it is worthy of remembrance that you can get a long way with a short back-swing by playing in the manner indicated. My own running-up mashie is my mongrel club. It is nearly straightfaced, and it is wonderfully useful for odd jobs. It gets me out of long grass; it keeps the ball low against the wind; it runs me up; it seems to be always coming in handy when no thoroughbred would meet the situation. A good mongrel club is a treasure.

Well, we have approached the hole in a variety of ways. It is high time that we were on the green.

CHAPTER VIII

PUTTING is a delicate matter, and I, of all people, ought to write about it in a delicate way. The reader of this book who has honoured me by noticing my doings on the links during recent years, and has observed my infinite capacity for missing little putts, may arrive at the conclusion that I lack nothing in presumptuousness when I offer instruction as to the best way of getting the ball into the hole from a short distance. Except, however, for emphasizing a few fundamental truths which are immutably correct, I do not intend to tell anybody how to putt. There are many ways of performing the operation successfully. I can claim, however, to be in a position to explain how not to putt. I think I know as well as anybody how not to do it.

Putting is, in a sense, a pastime distinct from golf. Half the secret of accomplishing it triumphantly lies, I suppose, in realizing that it is not very difficult. When driving or approaching, it is necessary for the player to remember certain established principles, and follow them to the letter if he would produce the desired result. There is one valuable precept which applies to putting as strongly as to any other shot in the

game.   That maxim is: "Keep the head still."
As regards stance and manner of hitting the ball,
it is for the individual to discover on the green
the means that suit him best with the club that
gives him most confidence.   The finest way to
putt is the way that gets the ball into the hole.
And confidence is half the battle.   Without it,
putting is not merely difficult; it is impossible.

The reader may not need to be reminded that,
of late years, I have often been lacking in that
valuable quality called confidence.   Especially has
this been the case in connexion with downright
easy putts—shots varying in length from six inches
to four or five feet.   Let me unburden my soul;
let me relate just what I have done wrongly on
hundreds of occasions, just why I have done it,
and just how I have sought to cure myself—
sought with some success, if I may judge by my
putting during the period in which this book was
written.

Perhaps it will be best if I reverse the order
of the ordeal, and start with the cure.   On
occasions I have gone on to the course in the
rapidly gathering gloom, when, in playing even
a short putt, the character of the ground between
the ball and the hole has been hard to distinguish.
I have seen the ball and the hole; and found
that I could nearly always put the former into
the latter—simply because, it seemed to me, I
had not worried to search for intervening difficulties.   If the golfer will adjourn to a green to
practise putting in the dusk of an evening, I feel
sure that he will find the whole business much
easier than it seems in the daytime.   With light
just sufficient to enable him to detect the dim outlines of the slopes, but not enough to give him
the opportunity of exaggerating their horrors,
he will discover himself putting with splendid

self-reliance and success. Care is essential; but
I firmly believe that, if you feel anxious and are
determined to look diligently for complications
along the line, you will find them all right,
even though they have no existence outside your
own mind.

That remark, however, merely serves to accentuate the inner peculiarity of putting, and its difference from any other department of the game.
In drives and iron shots, there are degrees of
prosperity. You may not hit your drive quite
properly, but you may still be on the course without serious loss of distance. The fate of a short
putt is an extreme; it is either perfect or ghastly.
There is no mediocrity, no chance of recovery.
That is why, I presume, the stroke is so trying;
it is so fateful. To be able to appreciate its intri-
cacies at precisely their correct value, and treat
them accordingly, is one of the secrets of successful putting. They must not be underrated, because sometimes they really are serious; but when
they insist upon presenting themselves in a porten-
tous way, the poor victim is a person to be pitied.
They get on his nerves to such an extent that
he simply cannot keep his head still during the
stroke. And so he fails. In the dusk, when the
survey of the line in minute detail is impossible,
putting really is easy. At least, so I have found
it. It is a strange remedy to get out in the gloom
in order to obtain confidence, but it is no stranger
than the disease.

I suppose that, at some time or other, nearly
everybody has suffered from incapacity within
four feet of the hole. In my own case, the attack
was painfully protracted; I can only hope that
I am justified in speaking of it now in the past
tense. I have never felt nervous when taking
part in a golf tournament; this lack of confidence

which overtook me when I played a short putt
was something altogether worse than nervous-
ness. As I stood addressing the ball, I would
watch for my right hand to jump. At the end of
about two seconds, I would not be looking at
the ball at all. My gaze would have become
riveted on my right hand. I simply could not
resist the desire to discover what it was going
to do. Directly I felt that it was about to jump,
I would snatch at the ball in a desperate effort
to play the shot before the involuntary movement
could take effect. Up would go my head and
body with a start, and off would go the ball—
anywhere but on the proper line. Such was the
outcome of a loss of confidence. I felt completely
comfortable with putts of three yards or more,
and could play them satisfactorily; it was when I
got to within four feet of the hole that I became
conscious of the difficulties, studied the line with
infinite particularity so as to leave nothing to
chance, and then watched my hand to see what
it was going to do. I could always tell when
I was about to have relief. If no jump visited
me on the first green, I knew that I was safe
for the round. As a generator of confidence, I
would recommend a course of putting in the dusk.
There is a lot of imagination in seeing a line all
the way from the ball to the hole.

Unquestionably the most important principle in
putting is to keep the head and body absolutely
still during the stroke. I know this from bitter
experience. Whenever I have been putting
badly, I have been moving my head (and therefore my body), and I am sure that the great
majority of failures on the green are traceable
to the same fault. The arms and wrists should
make the club act as a pendulum. The implement
should swing easily without causing the body to

move to the extent of even an eighth of an inch. If the clock swayed to and fro with the pendulum, it would not, I imagine, keep very good time. When you are putting, your head should be as still as the dial of the clock; your body should be as stable as the case. Your arms, wrists, and club should constitute the pendulum. Then you will keep good time. The methods of all good putters demonstrate the truth of this assertion— all, at least, save one. The inevitable exception to the rule is Tom Ball, who certainly does sway to some extent during the stroke. As he brings the club forward, his head and body move in the same direction, with the result that his left hip, which starts behind the ball, is in front of the object by the time that he plays the shot. Tom Ball is a very fine putter, and any golfer who possesses a characteristic on the green such as that described, and who thrives on it, is justified in his unorthodoxy. There is no truer saying than that which expresses the belief that putting is an inspiration, and it is certain that we do not all adopt the same pose in moments of inspiration. Consequently let the player putt in the way that suits him; the point that I am trying to emphasize is that it is not much use for the average golfer to try this body movement. In ninety-nine persons out of a hundred, it would be fatal. Accurate judgment of strength comes with practice; the chief difficulty is to make the ball travel in the proper direction. In nearly all cases, the missing of short putts is caused by the moving of the head. If you can summon the determination to continue looking at the spot where the ball has been for a second or two after you have struck it, you will not often miss a short putt. But the accomplishment of that feat of restraint simply means that you are possessed of confi-

PUTTING

dence; it means that you know that the ball has gone into the hole, so that you are not in a hurry to gaze at the result. The best way to encourage this comforting faith is to keep the head down till the finish of the follow-through.

Twelve or fifteen years ago, when putting never gave me the slightest trouble, I always played on the green a stroke which was simply a condensed form of the push-shot. I addressed the ball with the hands very slightly in front of it, imparted back-spin to it by the use of the wrists, and grazed the grass several inches in front of the spot from which the ball had been struck. That was when I employed a putting-cleek for the business. With the skittish rubber-cored ball, I do not fancy the push-shot on the green. I endeavour to play a pendulum stroke, which induces a steady follow-through with the arms—not the body. Taking it all round, that is perhaps the simplest and best means of attaining the end. With the help of Mr Arthur Brown I have devised for the purpose a club which, while it embraces the main points of nearly every well-known brand of putter, is distinct from anything else. I am frankly enthusiastic about it; its lie and balance seem to be such that one simply cannot help getting the ball into the hole with it. What this change means to a man who has undergone the torture which I have suffered on the green during recent years, I cannot adequately explain. It is heavenly. Only the player who has missed hundreds of holeable putts in a season is in a position to appreciate it. I cannot believe that my new friend is going to play me false. Such is the effect of confidence; the quality which, I know full well, has a way of coming and going without giving any reason.

The choice of grip, like that of club, must be

a matter of individual preference. It is desirable to have the two hands overlapping, or at least touching; for the rest, the player is well advised in holding the club in the manner that he fancies. Do not, however, allow the hands to be even a sixteenth of an inch apart on the shaft; the issue of such separation is nearly certain to be fatal. Since I saw Mr W. J. Travis play at Sandwich in 1904, I have always regarded his grip as theoretically the best one. So far as I can remember, what he does is to overlap with the first and second fingers of the left hand. He places those fingers over the third and little fingers of the right hand. It might be sufficient merely to put the forefinger of the left hand over the little finger of the right. I have tried this kind of hold, and done exceedingly well with it during periods of respite from the agony of watching for that wretched jump. If the reader will experiment with it, he will find that it very greatly reduces the danger of pushing the club away from the feet during the backward swing. It is one of the perils of putting, dependent as it is on the action of the arms and wrists that the right hand, which is essentially and naturally the putting hand, is apt to urge the club out in front instead of bringing it back in such a manner that it comes in a trifle towards the player. Mr Travis's grip seems to keep the right hand just sufficiently under control, and deter it from pursuing a wayward course. It may not suit all golfers, but in conception it is excellent.

The old maxim, "Never up, never in," is, I think, as valuable as ever. It is very easy to be too bold with the modern ball; but the man who is lacking in courage does not often win on the green. Nearly all good putters hit the ball with the utmost firmness. Watch, for instance, Tom

Ball. He gives the ball a hearty (although none the less rhythmic) clout, and does not often fail. There are players who like to cut their putts. Jack White is, however, the only consistently good putter I know who invariably adopts this principle. The great mass of evidence suggests that the best spin is that imparted by the pull, which is produced by turning the right hand over in a very slight degree at the moment of impact. Willie Park, one of the finest putters I have ever seen, always pulls; so does Arnaud Massy, another deadly man on the green. Personally, I try to hit the ball without either cut or pull.

One cannot justifiably be dogmatic where putting is concerned, except in regard to the few points on which I have insisted. So many men, so many methods—that is the whole of the subject. J. H. Taylor, who is a most accurate putter and a rare man for holing the ball at a pinch, seems to me to have improved since he adopted his own particular style of sticking out his left elbow so that it points almost straight towards the hole as he makes the address and plays the stroke. His hands are well in front of the ball all the while. James Braid, who seldom misses anything that is holeable, has a way of stopping for quite a long while at the top of the putting swing. He takes the club back, and there he pauses for an appreciable period, as though he were coolly determining not to be guilty of a snatched shot. And the better he is putting, the longer he waits at the top of his swing. Every good putter possesses individualism.

Personally, I do not believe in studying the line from its two ends. The player who examines the situation first from the ball and then from the hole is likely to see two lines. He finds him-

self filled with philosophic fears and speculative
doubts. The harvest that he reaps is so rich
that he is distracted by it.   He borrows a bit
from one line and a bit from the other, and
finishes where Fortune and a baffling complexity
of slopes may take him.   As I have said previously, there is a lot of imagination in seeing a
line.   In fact, it is nearly all imagination.   If we
take our " nightcap " in the form of ten minutes'
putting in the dusk, we shall hole out with ease.
We shall not see alarming undulations, which,
the more we study them, the more they seem to
demand infinitesimal estimation.   We shall simply
inspect the hole and the ball, and bring them
close together.   I sometimes think that with putts
of a yard or four feet, it would be best if, without
more than a cursory look at the line, we were to
walk up to the ball and unaffectedly knock it into
the hole.   That is a counsel of perfection; it is
just the system of George Duncan, and other wise
appreciators of the difficulties of the short putt.
But when all has been said, the fact remains
that the work on the green is governed by the
mood of the player.   Once I hit upon the idea
of trying a putter about a foot long.   I took it
over to La Boulie to use in the French open
championship, and did very well with it for two
rounds.   So far as I can recollect, I was leading
very comfortably at the end of thirty-six holes.
Early in the third round I was presented with a
putt of no more than six inches.   My right hand
jumped; I went about two feet past the hole, and
my partner, who was a Frenchman, gave vent to
a very deliberate and wholesomely English—
" Good Heavens! "   I finished that round putting
with an iron, and with a good deal of iron in my
soul.
Putting is so much a matter of confidence that

I sometimes think that the average player ought to be better at it than the champion. I say this with the knowledge that it looks remarkably like an excuse in pickle, but I believe that, when a man has a reputation to defend, the task of getting the ball into the hole from a comparatively short distance is more difficult than anything else in the game. In this connection I remember an incident that occurred at St Andrews a few years ago, when a tournament open to amateurs and professionals was decided. In the semi-final, Alexander Herd met an amateur, who holed putts from all parts of the green. The amateur generally had the worst of the play up to the green; then he would get down a long putt, and leave Herd struggling for a half. The match was even at the seventeenth hole. At the eighteenth Herd won. Then he turned on his pertinacious rival. "Look here," he said, "you wouldn't hole the putts you've been holing to-day if you had to do it for your living." There was a lot of truth in that remark. Putting ought to be easy to amateurs; it is necessarily much more difficult to professionals, because their reputations are apt to depend upon it. Keep your head still, swing pendulum fashion with the arms and wrists, follow-through, and don't look up as you do it. These hints—and a recognition of the presumed fact that you are going to hole the ball—are the guides to happiness on the green.

CHAPTER IX

RECOVERING FROM DIFFICULTIES

L ET us be bunkered. For a very long while we have delayed the evil happening. We have played many shots with a variety of clubs; even have we putted. We may, indeed, have arrived at the conclusion that the task of tapping the ball into the hole is easy. It is so occasionally. If we happen to have developed such a spirit of triumphal elation, perhaps it is time that we began to look on the dark side of things. Self-reliance is good, but exultation is often fatal to the person engaged in a golf match. Paradise may descend upon him, but it has a way of flitting without notice. It leaves him in a cold, hard world, which is all the more trying because of the joy of the preceding minutes—precious minutes to the golfer. Let him remember therefore, that there is always the possibility of his having to approach a shot with chastened feelings. At the most unexpected period, the cold, hard world may claim him as its own; that little world with steep sides and a base of sand, or—worse still—miserable clay.

When we make our way into a bunker in order to extract our errant ball from its clutches, we can possess no more suitable spirit than that of dignified chastenment. Personally, I have long since come to the conclusion that it is unwise to entertain any notion about performing heroics in hazards. The best thing to do is to look for the easiest way out, and take the line of least resistance. There are, naturally, situations in which we must endeavour to accomplish an almost superhuman feat, as, for instance, when the opposition is twelve inches from the hole in the same number of shots that we have expended in making the acquaintance of the bunker; but in ordinary circumstances there is no scheme more profitable —or perhaps I should say less unprofitable—than that of searching for the simplest means of escape and trusting to the saving of a stroke in the short game in order to avert the loss of the hole. And the more moderate the player, the more strongly is this policy to be recommended. I really believe that many a long-handicap man regularly tries to accomplish greater deeds with a niblick and a half-buried ball than any first-class golfer would dream of attempting. My advice to the bunkered player is—" Don't be greedy; be content to get out."

I need scarcely say that these remarks are based on the assumption that we are about to play a real bunker shot. The ball is nestling down in the sand, or other yielding substance, in such a way that we cannot see the bottom of it. When Providence presents us with a good lie in a bunker; when the ball is teed-up, or, at any rate, poised with some degree of lofty bearing, then we can pick it up cleanly with the club that seems most suited to the occasion, having regard to the nearness of the face of the hazard, and try for distance. As I will explain in a subsequent chapter, professionals generally play the push-shot in such circumstances. For the present, however, let us

consider that we are endeavouring to rescue the
ball from an exceedingly unpleasant place.

We must fix our eye on a spot an inch and a
half or two inches behind the ball, and determine
to delve right into the bunker—as far into it as
we can penetrate—with a forcible blow of the niblick.   We shall need a full swing for the purpose.
It can be as full a swing as for the drive, but it
must be a considerably more upright one because
we want to dig the ball out of its retreat.   There
should be no element of the sweeping action
about this stroke.   The player should turn his
body well towards the direction in which he wants
to go (a stance a little more open than that for
the mashie shot); take the club up fairly straight
to the top of the swing, and bring it down
vehemently into the sand an inch and a half or
two inches behind the ball, throwing his body
slightly forward and nearly all his weight on to
the left leg at the moment of the stab.   He need
not worry at all about nicety of touch—that is,
when he is really badly bunkered.   The club
should not come into contact with the ball at any
part of the stroke   The player must determine
to make a mighty cleft in the sand—or whatever
the substance may be—behind the ball, whereupon
the latter will be forced out of its ensconced
position and often hurled a considerable distance.
Do not trouble about a follow-through.   The
effort should finish with the club-head buried in the
bunker.   All that you are trying to do is to create
such a disturbance at the back of the ball as will
cause that object to move out of the hazard, and
when the niblick has made its way into the
selected spot, it will have done its work.

The less distance you want to go, the more
sand you take.   The point here made hardly
needs emphasizing.   You must always hit hard

Stance for the niblick shot

BUNKERED

Top of the swing for the niblick. The weight has shifted over to the left leg rather than the right, so that the club may be brought down to dig forcibly into the soil

in a bunker (that is a golden rule), and it is obvious that the farther you dig behind the ball, the less the latter object will be influenced by the disturbance. Sometimes you have to excavate as though you were starting to make a grave for yourself. I must confess that on a strange course a shot in a bunker often partakes of the character of a speculation, since there is little opportunity of telling the consistency of the foundation. When a first-class player takes two strokes to recover from a hazard, it is generally because he has failed accurately to estimate the density of the substance. He has aimed too far behind the ball. Nobody is allowed to ground the club, or in any way test the nature of the base, and even the man of experience sometimes forms a wrong judgment. It is not often that the person of long and varied observation misses his first shot in a hazard through an attempt to do too much with a half-buried ball. His fault is usually the modest one of trying to do too little. My own watchword when I am badly bunkered is " Moderation " (of ambition as well as language). It pays in the end.

In the chapter concerning the mashie, I have mentioned the danger of endeavouring to lift the ball into the air on the face of the club. The same warning may be proclaimed in regard to bunker shots. Far better is it to dig down behind the object with all your might, than to try to push the niblick under the ball and lift it up with the club. The sand—or even harder stuff—if agitated in the right place, and with plenty of power, will nearly always release its victim. When the ball is close to the face of the hazard, it is often possible to play a cut shot in just the same way as with the mashie. The lie for this purpose must be a good one, but granted such a favour, the

H

shot is well worth trying by the golfer of some accomplishment. Frequently it enables him to reach the green without a further expenditure of strokes. Naturally, a line to the left must be taken (in such circumstances he will generally have to escape sideways whether he decide to try the cut or simply perform the stab), and there must be, as with the mashie, a distinct attempt to draw the club across the ball after an upward swing in which the arms have pushed the implement slightly away from the body. This, however, is only a stroke for a peculiar situation—a good lie near the face of the bunker guarding the green. In the ordinary way the game is to bury the niblick forcefully behind the ball. Do not be afraid of burying it too deep; you cannot go too far into the sand. It is often possible to obtain in this manner a shot of very useful length.

Even in clay, as, for instance, in dry ditches, the tactics here described can be practised; although as clay is usually fairly dense and resistive, it is necessary in such circumstances to aim only a little way behind the ball, say, from half an inch to an inch. If you try to take two or three inches of this tenacious earth, you may get it all right on the face of the implement, but without urging the ball clear of the hazard. Still, unless you feel that the opportunity is excellent for making a cleanly-hit shot, the thing to do is to dig. I have very seldom seen soil so hard that it cannot be excavated, although sometimes a great amount of vigour is necessary. I shall never forget a wonderful shot which Joshua Taylor played in a distinctly clayey ditch at Clacton-on-Sea. He must have buried the head of his niblick nearly a foot below the surface, but the ball came out all right. Indeed, if I remember aright, he laid it dead.

A frequently seen but incorrect method of playing a niblick shot. It is a scoop—an attempt to carry the ball on the club—which generally speaking, is impossible

BUNKERED

Finish of the niblick shot, with the club remaining in the soil

Sometimes on courses of more or less ancient architecture, the ball is found tucked up against the back of a bunker. On modern courses such a situation is scarcely ever presented, because the twentieth-century method of making bunkers is to go down almost straight for several feet in forming the back of the hazard. The whole of the bunker is below the surface of the ground, and its depth is much the same at all parts. This is unquestionably the best principle, inasmuch as a ball which just trickles into the hazard slides down the precipitous back wall and runs sufficiently far forward to give its proprietor a chance of getting at it with a club. It is one of the tendencies of the day, this inclination to use the underground regions; we go down a lift into the bowels of the earth in order to travel in a tube, and we find our up-to-date golfing trouble below the surface. The old type of bunker began almost level with the ground; and it was completed by the erection of a bank on the far side. There are thousands of these bunkers still in existence, and when the ball just trickles into one of them so that it lies close up against the shallow back wall, the position is absurdly unhappy. Sometimes it is necessary to cut right through the several inches of turf in order to execute the stab shot. It is occasionally the only alternative to playing out sideways. And none of us like to pursue our golf as the crab walks or the donkey goes up a hill; it seems so utterly unheroic to tack off the appointed line. Still, I would not discourage the moderate golfer from adopting the safer course of poking his way out to either flank when he finds himself hemmed in at the back. His dominant determination ought to be to recover in one stroke. If he can get a long way out, well and good; if the situation is at all involved, let him be content to struggle clear of it by a matter of a few yards, and offer thanks for such a small mercy, provided always that it is procurable at a cost of no more than one stroke. It is a foible of the average golfer that, when he has taken six at a simple hole in a medal competition, a bunkered shot at the next hole often ruins his card beyond all chance of redemption. The reason is simply that he tries to do something wonderful in the hazard so as not to be debited with another six. The reward often comes as a shock; he gets a seven instead of a six.

When the ground is very hard, it is sometimes a blessing in disguise to be in a bunker near the green. If you know your bunker (know that it is not of a nature that wreaks awful vengeance upon the visitant), and are on good terms with your niblick, it is frequently better to be in the sand than on the grass. This remark is not mere philosophy; it is good advice. After a drought, it may be very difficult to make the ball stop on the green, even though you play a good approach from the fairway. If you know how to execute a bunker shot, you can take so much sand as to put an inevitable check on the ball and make it rise so sluggishly as to stop somewhere near the hole. In some circumstances it is safer when playing a long shot up to the green to hug the wing hazards, and even get into one of them, than to send the ball straight up the middle and risk a lot of trouble beyond the hole.

In this connexion, the peculiarities of the seventeenth—the famous " Road " hole—at St Andrews at once occur to the mind. When the ground is hard, the ordinary game is to put the second shot at the foot of the slope in front of the green, run up, and hope for a four, while feeling satisfied to take five. But if you want to adopt bold tactics, it is better to go to the left in spite of the bunker that is there awaiting you, than to play straight and submit yourself to the danger of finishing on the dreaded road, whence in all probability you will simply return to the bunker. This latter hazard is an excellent one in which to execute a niblick-burying shot behind the ball. There is a good chance of getting dead from it, or sufficiently near the hole to obtain a four. They say that when Braid was in that bunker in the third round of the open championship of 1910, the Jubilee championship which he won so brilliantly, he took something like a bucketful of sand in order to play a shot of a few yards. People who were present declare that the very green trembled when his club crashed into the hazard. A good golfer knows exactly what to do in a bunker; nobody can be quite sure with the rubber-cored ball of the best means of playing an approach off an adamantine surface on to a green of similar hardness. One effect of the introduction of the resilient ball has been to make bunkers very useful as places of temporary refuge near the green.

I know that I have not infrequently made my way deliberately into them in order to have the chance of laying the next shot dead. When Braid and I were partners against Duncan and Mayo at Walton Heath a few years ago, I was not afraid of putting my confrère into the bunker on the left of the fifth green. I did so in each round. I knew that from there he was sure to get close to the hole. He did not fail. We won it each time. We are not all so strong as Braid, who can recover from anything; but, under certain conditions, there is something to be gained by considering whether the " trouble," as it is called, can be used to advantage. I remember another foursome decided on a course of indifferent quality, in which my partner and I decided to play into the rough at certain holes. The lies were better there than on the clayey, rain-sodden fairway. We gained an easy victory, but some of the papers remarked on the following day that our golf had not been very good because we had been off the line so often! There was method in our crookedness.

Now that the "humps and hollows" have become so popular (or, at least, as popular as places of retribution can hope to be), a bunker shot is sometimes presented where no bunker exists. When your ball is at the foot of a high mound which is in the direct line to the hole, and right under your nose in such a way as to prevent anything in the nature of a following-through stroke, the only means to the end is to stab behind the ball in just the same manner as in sand, and make the soil produce the desired lofty effect. This, however, can only be done when the grass is short. The distance which you aim behind the ball must be governed by the nature of the turf; in any case, it will not be so great as in sand. An inch will generally suit the occasion; the point to remember is to dig the niblick into the ground, as you would do in sand, and bury it. Otherwise you will not often get the ball over the mound owing to the unavoidable arrestation of the swing. A sequential point to recollect is to tread down the turf which you have uplifted. Where you have gone others may follow.

In playing this stab shot, it is a great help to throw the body slightly forward and nearly all the weight on to the left leg as the club burrows its way forcibly into the earth. In long grass it is impossible to bury the niblick. This particular tool will do a lot of things, and maintain its integrity in times of rough treatment, which

even a sledge-hammer might resent; but it will
not cut straight down into very long grass and
at the same time perform the important operation
of making the ball rise. When the grass is rank
and an earthen bank confronts the player (a situation that often presents itself in what are sometimes called grass bunkers) tactics different from
those employed in an ordinary bunker are demanded. The only feasible plan is to aim several
inches behind the ball; cut the grass at the roots
with a following-through stroke; and throw the
body back at the instant of impact with nearly all
the weight on to the right leg. In grass that is
positively formidable in length and thickness, it
is always necessary to aim well behind the ball
(sometimes as much as four or five inches), so as
to slice off the herbage at the roots before reaching the ball. There are occasions when the grass
comes up in bunches, and flies round your head
as though you were being crowned queen (or
king) of the May. This, however, is the way to
recover. If you are merely in very long grass
with no lofty obstacle immediately in front, naturally you will not throw your body back as the
club reaches the ball. In such circumstances you
should have the weight equally divided. It is
still important, however, to aim some little way
behind the ball and cut right along the roots of
the grass, instead of coming down to the object
and trying to scoop it out of its entanglement.
The stems have a way of arranging themselves
around the ball as though determined to defend
it till the last gasp. They must be cut away in
the manner described. In gorse, as in long
grass, it is necessary to aim well behind the ball,
and cut through the bush. It is hefty work; I
wish you little of it.

These, then, are the general principles of the

business of recovering from difficulties.   I do not desire to urge that no other schemes are correct.   There are a hundred and one different positions that threaten disaster, and a hundred and one different ways of escaping.   Much must be left to the judgment of the player, and to his knowledge of his own powers.   The shots that I have described are applicable to those distressing situations of the everyday type.   They are sufficient; let us end this chapter of accidents and proceed to happier themes.

CHAPTER X

THE "PUSH" SHOT

THERE comes a period when our golf shows unmistakable evidence of improvement; a soul-satisfying time when we entertain no serious doubt as to our ability to execute a plain shot in the correct way. The hardest part of the golfer's life is that stage in his novitiate when his only faith is in his capacity for foozling. He swings beautifully without the ball, but directly that object is placed in front of him, the difficulties of hitting it properly rush into his mind like a raging torrent. For the first second he wonders whether he will succeed. Before he has finished addressing the ball, his sentiments present a mixture of resignation and desperate hope. That is the period when instruction by voice has an excellent moral effect. The professional may do nothing more than say repeatedly:—"You'll hit it all right if you do what I tell you"; but those words seem to breed a lot of confidence in the doubter. I must confess, however, that the instructor occasionally has to exercise a lot of restraint in order to produce the desired results. I once knew a man who constantly needed this vocal encouragement, and who invariably raised a side-issue by saying in response:—"Yes; but if I hit it, I'm sure to

121

laugh so much that I shan't be able to do it again." That was very trying. It is easy enough to tell a person not to move his head, but to tell him not to laugh for joy at his triumphs seems almost inhuman. The worst of it was that he had good ground for fear as to the danger of his risible tendencies. Whenever he made a good shot, he was so elated, and he laughed so gaily about it, that it was out of the question to expect him to do anything equally satisfactory for quite a long while.

Sooner or later, however, the earnest golfer attains that degree of proficiency when he knows that the accomplishment of an ordinary stroke is within his power. His mistrust in his own abilities (that greatest and most natural handicap of the novice) has disappeared. Now is the time for him to start learning what is, I think, the most valuable shot in golf. It is called the push-shot.

I suppose it is true that the standard of amateur golf has fallen below that of professional golf. Mr H. H. Hilton very nearly beat all of us in the open championship at Sandwich in 1911, and I have poignant recollections of waiting for an hour round the home green while he was engaged in an effort which was very perturbing to me in particular; but, save for that performance by a truly great player, the data provided during recent years support the general impression that the leading professionals have maintained a higher degree of skill than the leading amateurs. There have been many discussions as to the reason for this state of affairs. I venture to say, that the explanation is to be found almost exclusively in the fact that the professionals make the most of the push-shot. That is the great secret of their success, and if amateurs would practise that stroke more assiduously, I believe that the disparity between the two sections of the golfing community would be greatly lessened.   Some amateurs do play the push-shot, and play it well. But they are a small company; the great majority do not appreciate either its scientific beauties or its practical possibilities. The professionals resort to it in many situations, and find it invaluable. They even play it with a niblick in bunkers, when the ball is lying cleanly.   Sometimes you will hear a spectator remark when following a couple of professionals : — "I can't imagine how these fellows manage to get so far out of bunkers." The push-shot is the solution to the mystery.   Its feature on all occasions when it is properly executed is that it makes the ball rise sharply, and yet prevents it from flying high, and so losing distance.   It is clear that we could not hope for a ball played out of a bunker to behave in a manner better than that indicated.   We want it to ascend quickly, so as to escape the face of the hazard; we also want it to go a long way.   The push-shot compels it to do these two things.   The back-spin is the influence that works for so much good.   For a moment after the impact, that spin is so powerful that the ball, revolving rapidly in the direction opposite to that in which it is travelling, necessarily goes up sharply into the air.   It is trying to whirl back, as it were, to the player; but the power of the forward movement is too much for it.   The conflict of the two forces naturally causes it to rise sharply.   Almost immediately, however, they come to an amicable understanding.   The ball. having been struck cleanly with anything up to a three-quarter swing, insists upon going forward.   It cannot be denied. But the velocity of the impact having been spent, the back-spin makes the shot "flatten out" so to

speak. So, again, we have the two influences
operating in unison for the good of the player.
The ball must necessarily go in the direction in
which it has been hit; but the spin keeps it low
and, moreover, maintains its flight in one plane
for an astonishingly long time. On and on it
goes until its power is spent; then it drops as
sharply as it has risen, and runs very few yards.
It is wonderful how far one can get out of a
bunker by playing this shot with a niblick. As
I have previously mentioned, the ball must be
lying cleanly; if it be even slightly buried, the
stroke which is the subject of this chapter cannot
be considered within the range of practical
politics. However, we are not supposed to make
the acquaintance of bunkers. Human nature
being frail, we do come into contact with them
at intervals, so that it is necessary to consider
the best way of emerging triumphantly from their
grasp; but it is more comforting when discussing
the push-shot, to suppose that we are always on
the fairway. By a skilful golfer who practises it
assiduously, it can be executed successfully and
profitably with any club. James Braid often plays
it from the tee with his driver. Not long ago I
had thirty-six holes with him at Walton Heath.
Nothing in my golfing life has impressed me more
than the way in which Braid executed the push-
shot with all kinds of clubs on that occasion. I
honestly do not think that he has any equal at it.
It is my own favourite stroke (in the days of the
gutta-percha ball I simply worshipped it, and
made myself, I think, pretty good at it), but I
fear I do not often play it now as I played it in
former days. It is the master stroke in the game,
and is worthy the earnest study of every golfer
who is approaching the region of scratch form.
It demands great accuracy and a perfect synchro-

nization of several unusual movements, but it is within the reach of anybody who has confidence in his ability to perform a shot properly. It comes with diligent practice.   The person of medium handicap may find that he possesses the knack of doing it.   If not, I would recommend him to perfect himself at the plain strokes before tackling the more intricate ones.

I have emphasized the fact that the push-shot can be accomplished with any club in the bag, inasmuch as there seems to be a common impression that it should never be attempted with anything but a cleek or an iron.   Often one reads or hears that So-and-so is very skilful at the push-shot with the cleek.   Assuming the criticism to be sound, the chances are that the aforementioned So-and-so is equally clever at the push-shot with the iron or mashie, or niblick.   Certainly the professionals play it with all their iron clubs; and Braid, as I have already said, resorts to it with his driver when he wants to prevent his tee shot from running far.   A complete mastery over the stroke raises the golfer from the stage of ordinary excellence to the plane in which he is distinguished; that is why it is so well worth studying.

While it is a shot for any club, the cleek is perhaps the best implement with which to begin practising it.   Before proceeding to describe how it is done, let me explain in a few words the idea of the stroke.   What happens (at least, so I feel convinced, although nobody sees it happen) is that the ball is made to spin slightly up the face of the club at the instant of impact.   The golfer has no need to worry about producing this effect; it will come if he accomplish the shot properly. That is the essence of the shot; it produces the back-spin while the power of the blow naturally sends the ball forward. Now as to the way to obtain the effect; a way that must be precise, although it is not nearly so difficult a problem as it may look on paper. The swing must be distinctly more upright than for the ordinary cleek shot. The club must go up straighter than for any other stroke in the game, and, that being so, nothing more than a three-quarter swing should be permitted. The uprightness of the swing will demand a closer stance than for the ordinary cleek shot. The player should be several inches nearer to the ball because, instead of swinging the club round to it with a purely propelling action, he is going to endeavour to come down on to the side of the ball, if I may so explain it. This sounds, I know, only about one degree removed from an incentive to topping. It is likely that the golfer will go through a period of that painful purgatory in his early efforts to execute the shot, but it will be solely attributable to his failure to use his body and wrists in the correct way at the time of impact. It is quite clear that the simple propelling influence will not produce the essential back-spin. The face of the club must come down broadside on to the ball so as to make the latter run up the face of the implement, thus imparting the spin while the forward movement is in progress.

We left ourselves standing closer to the ball than for the ordinary cleek. The stance, too, should be distinctly more forward. In no circumstances should the hands be behind the ball during the address; indeed, they must be an inch or two in front of it. Moreover, the eyes must be focussed, not on the turf immediately behind the object, but on that extremity of the ball itself which is farthest from the hole. During the address, our range of vision, so far as we are

THE "PUSH" CLEEK SHOT

Stance. The most noticeable feature of it is that the hands are slightly forward

Top of the swing

conscious of it, should end half-way down the ball—on the pimple that is protruding farthest away from the hole (if we are using a ball of pimple marking). When we play an ordinary cleek shot, we graze the turf several inches behind the ball so as to make the loft of the club do its work immediately. With the push-shot, we obtain the loft in a different way. In an infinitesimal period something happens which produces back-spin before the action of raising the ball has time to take effect. What we want to do is to bring the instrument down so that the hindmost part of the ball is struck at a point of the club's face which is rather nearer to the sole than the top. In a way, then, we want to come down half on top of the ball. We have seen that our hands are in front of it, so that when the contact is made at the rearmost part of the ball (not under it), more than half of the club as between the sole and the top is tilted, so to speak, over the ball. I need scarcely say that this position is of the shortest instant's duration. We are not going to stand and reflect on it; we have no time even to catch a glimpse of it. Nevertheless, the securing of it is the first essential of the shot; this is a fact upon which I imagine all good exponents of the push-stroke have satisfied themselves.

Now as to the simultaneous yet rhythmic movements which complete the shot. At the moment of impact (right at that instant; not the smallest fraction of a second earlier or later) the player should straighten the elbows, stiffen the wrists, and let the body go forward a few inches with the club. The quick action of the elbows and wrists will push the face of the club under the ball as both go forward, and the body moving slightly in the same direction will assist in the project. The ground will be grazed the smallest distance imaginable in front of the place where the ball was reposing. The follow-through should not be arrested; indeed, it should be encouraged, because the wrists and elbows must relax to the normal the instant they have executed the push; but, in the ordinary way, the follow-through will not be so full as in ordinary shots.

I need scarcely say that the secret of success is to make the various movements synchronize to perfection. The arms must straighten, the wrists must tighten, and the body must move forward at the exact time when the club meets the ball. The effect will be readily perceived. The club-face will be turned under the ball, while picking it up cleanly. The two will be in contact for a period not long enough to be noticed, but sufficiently appreciable for the ball to run up the face of the implement as it is being urged forward. Thus will be produced the back-spin. A tight grip is necessary, and I may perhaps repeat the warning that directly the impact is complete the elbows and wrists should relax so as to facilitate the follow-through. They will have done their work.

This description may make the shot appear like a piece of jugglery, but it is a faithful explana--tion of the stroke as I play it myself, and as I have seen others play it. From time to time I have observed in responsible papers articles dealing with the push-shot, and giving wrong impressions of its character. Thus I have read on more than one occasion that rudimentary mechanics prove beyond all question that, in order to raise a ball into the air and obtain an accurate and adequate flight, it is necessary for the club to make impact below the centre of the ball. I do not profess to know much about the science of

Finish. The straightening of the elbows at the moment of the impact
has naturally made the club finish above the head (as it should do
for this shot) instead of behind it

THE " PUSH " CLEEK SHOT

Finish for a long shot

A DISTINCTION WITH A DIFFERENCE

The ordinary cleek shot. The turf has been taken behind the ball, as will be seen from the chalk-mark on which the ball was resting

The push shot with the cleek from a similar chalk-mark. The turf has been taken in front of the spot on which the ball rested mechanics, but I am sure that I know how the push-shot is played. If, at the outset, you were to strike the ball below the centre, you would not impart much back-spin to it. You might obtain a little, but the effort would be hardly distinguishable from an ordinary lofting shot. What you have to do is to bring the face of the club down to the ball at the centre of its mass, and then, by that simultaneous stiffening of the elbows, tightening of the wrists, and pushing forward of the body, make the face of the implement run almost half-way round the ball. It has been said that it is impossible for me or anybody else to observe what happens at the instant when the club and the ball come into contact. I am free to confess that it is impossible to see the club hit the ball. Let me, however, discuss the matter from another standpoint. A good player always knows what he is trying to do no matter what club he has in his hands. If he repeatedly hits the shots just as he tries to hit them, he knows that he is using the club and striking the ball in just the manner that he has conceived for the occasion. Otherwise we should have to arrive at the conclusion that all his satisfactory strokes were flukes, because he had endeavoured to accomplish the thing in a certain way and had obtained the desired result by unwittingly doing something else. That, surely, would be absurd. Consequently, although it is true that I do not see the club hit the ball, I know that the push-shot is obtained in the manner which I have described. I have dealt fully with the subject, and endeavoured to correct wrong impressions, because I feel that the " push " is now the master shot in golf, and the stroke which all good amateurs ought to practise if they take to heart the frequent reproach that the standard of their play is falling below that of professional golf.

I

CHAPTER XI

I T is a great advantage to have learnt your golf
(or to go and learn it) by the sea. Students
of the game's history will not need to be informed
that nearly all the leading players secured their
early training in the pastime on seaside links, or,
at any rate, at high and exposed places which the
four winds of heaven had claimed among their
own playgrounds The best school of experience
is a school in which that gentleman who is
known as old Boreas tries to assert authority.
Naturally, we do not want half a gale to prevail
every time we go out for a round (indeed, humanity is so frail that, if it had any say in the matter,
it might vote for the complete suppression of
atmospheric disturbance in the region of golf
courses), but the fact remains that repeated sub-
jection to a stiff wind helps more than any other
influence to make a person a finished golfer.
Cricketers and footballers may rise quickly to
fame from beginnings made in almost any circumstances—in suburban parks, on patches of waste
ground in busy industrial districts, anywhere. An
aptitude for golf can hardly fail to make itself
manifest at some time or other, and blessed is he
who possesses it; but twice blessed is he who has

the opportunity to develop it early in life on seaside links. For then necessity will make him the
father of invention. There is generally some
degree of commotion in the air by the sea, and
it has to be circumvented. Not always is it that
a plain, straightforward shot achieves the purpose. Ingenuity is stimulated; spin has sometimes to be imparted to the ball so that the wind
may be mastered. Then it is that the player
learns the higher science of golf; learns how to
compel the ball to do anything. When he takes
up his abode inland, he may have to practise
several new shots (the turf for one thing is generally quite different from that to which he has been
accustomed), but with his seaside training he can
overcome any difficulty. When a strong wind
arises, as it does at times in even the most shel-
tered places, he is unruffled by it, while the lifelong habitué of the course is perhaps buffeted
about in every direction. When, even in the
absence of wind, the need presents itself of doing
something unusual so as to make the ball curl
round an obstacle and reach the chosen spot, the
player from the nursery by the sea is usually
equal to the occasion.

The main principles of executing the pull or
slice are the same, no matter for what purpose
the shot is attempted. If you have hooked your
drive, and can only reach the green with your
second stroke by means of a sliced shot round an
obstruction, the method of securing that slice is
the same as when you are trying to juggle with
the wind, so that its strength, combined with spin
which you have imparted to the ball, may result in
the latter starting off the line and coming back
to it. Where the obstacle is concerned, you
probably do not want to come back to the line;
you simply require a slice so as to atone for the

pull—or vice versa. In the other case, the wind alone will influence the course of your ball, and the latter will have been sent off the line, so that, with the help of the elements and the spin, it shall return to the proper track without having been robbed of distance. It follows, then, that there are many degrees of slice and pull, according to circumstances. Only experience can teach the golfer just what degree is required for each situation that presents itself.

It is wind that provokes the most frequent demand for the exercise of these shots. If you find yourself confronted by a source of embarrassment which cannot be carried (a spinney, a house, or something like that), you may have to impart a quick slice or pull, or delay the effect of the spin so that the ball travels for a considerable distance in an almost straight line before the influence of the communicated whirl comes into operation. The player is naturally governed in these matters by the distance which he finds himself from the obstacle, but the fundamental features of the methods of accomplishing sliced or pulled shots are the same in all circumstances. If the golfer knows how to stand and how to use his right hand, a most important hand in this connexion for a particular degree of pull or slice, diligent practice ought to make him capable of attaining any other degree which he may require. The ability will come instinctively once he is master of the main idea. It is best to learn the shots in a wind, because then you have the whole world into which to aim, and, what is more, the wind assists in producing the desired effects. You seem to feel that it has come out to be friendly; that it is going to act in a positively benign way towards your scientific efforts. That is much more inspiring than sallying forth on a calm day with a determination to execute slices or pulls round such an inert institution as a collection of trees or a building.

These are all strokes for players of ability; the beginner may well regard them as distant objects of his ambition. Anybody, however, who feels tolerably certain of hitting a ball cleanly is justified in attempting the intentional slice or pull. Indeed, it is his duty to do so; otherwise, he is paying a very poor compliment to the scope of golf. Practical acquaintance with the subject will teach the player how many yards he should hit the ball off the straight line in order to gain his end. In fact, he needs to store up a knowledge of winds which would be a credit to the skipper of a sailing vessel. The danger of going too far off the line is always worthy of recollection; it is a downright tragedy when the intentional slice or pull meets with the fate of the unintentional one.

I have come to the conclusion that, when a strong wind blows from right to left, that is to say, from the slice side of the course to the pull side, it is a very risky procedure to hit a rubber-cored ball into the wind with pull on it so that it may come back to the middle of the course. It is nice if you can do it, and I know that, in the conditions described the great majority of good golfers attempt it. All the same it is hazardous. A ball with "draw" on it naturally runs farther than any other; its trajectory is low, and at the finish, it is spinning in such a way as to scamper gaily over the ground, aided and abetted by the wind. That is the danger of it. Unless the golfer is very skilful, unless he possesses a particularly fine power of discrimination in judging the force of the elements and selecting the place of descent, the resilient rubber-cored ball will very likely swing round at such a pace, and with such a spin on it when the wind takes command of it, as to run right across the fairway and into a bunker or the rough on the other side. Then, indeed, will he have sown the wind and reaped the whirlwind. It needs the very greatest delicacy of judgment and accuracy of action to play to perfection this pulled shot into half a gale of wind. When it is performed successfully, it gains a lot of ground, for it is the longest of all strokes; but, personally, I do not think that under modern conditions it is worth risking. A few golfers possess the instinct which enables them to execute it triumphantly nearly every time they try it, but I am sure that the majority would be wise if they resolved to abandon it. It may seem a proper and profitable undertaking to aim with pull into a right-to-left wind in order to make the latter help in the cause, but too often it means a scuttle of the ball across the course (especially when the fairway is narrow) and a fate that seems outrageous. This, at least, is the conclusion which I have reached after seeing the shot played many hundreds of times, and after playing it myself.

The above remarks contradict, I know, my old views on the subject; but the game has altered a lot in a few years. I used to recommend the policy (which is even now an easy favourite) of striking into the wind and imparting " draw " to the ball. That system could be attempted with safety when the ball was a less lively creation than it is at the present time. It can be tried now on soil more or less heavy, but when the turf accentuates the run, as it does, I suppose, at most times during the spring, summer, and autumn, such a shot in tempestuous circumstances is beset with danger. What I always do is to aim very slightly to the left (just one small degree in the same direction as that in which the wind is blow-ing), and communicate slice to the ball. The initial velocity of the shot prevents the wind from mastering it. Then when its strength is dying, the spin begins to exert influence, curls the ball into the wind, and brings it down quickly into the middle of the course with little run on it. I am free to confess that the distance to be obtained in this way is not so great as in the case of a pulled stroke, but the policy of the slice is by far the more trustworthy. It is better to lose a few yards and be safe, than to make a stroke of prodigious length into a bad place. In a powerful wind, the slice is easier to regulate than the pull, which sometimes defies perfect adjustment, so exaggerated are the effects of the very slightest error of omission or commission. Therefore, my advice to the golfer who desires to consistently conquer a turbulent air (and, incidentally, his opponent) is to pin his faith to the cut stroke. I believe that in nine cases out of ten, it will pay where the up-to-date ball is concerned.

In playing for the slice, the stance should be open—the ball about opposite to the toes of the left foot, which should be pointing outwards, and the right foot advanced so that the executant finds himself well behind the ball. The feet ought to be about the same distance apart as for the ordinary stroke; the first important matter is to dispose them so that they produce an open stance. Every golfer must discover for himself just what degree of openness he needs, but it will always be something more than the ordinary, because he is going to aim in some measure to the left of the line (that measure depending upon the strength of the wind) and make the ball curl back into the proper path. Now as to the manner of producing this latter effect. I suppose that there is more than one way of doing it. Some people say,

"Keep the right shoulder down and trust to
the swing to bring the face of the club across
the ball." This is not necessarily sufficient. Personally, I have a method which may—or may not
—be different from that employed by the majority
of players. I have not so very long satisfied myself thoroughly as to how I secure the slice. Now
I am convinced about it. With the weight mostly
on the right foot, I take the club up in an outward
direction in just the same way as for the cut mashie
shot. There is the same slight sway up to the
point where the elbows bend, and then as the
club comes back behind the head, the latter returns
to the proper position. At the top of the swing,
in that immeasurably small period when one braces
oneself for the effort, I give my body a sharp turn
at the hips—a turn of a few inches towards the
hole. That action makes my downward swing the
corollary of my upward swing where the intentional slice is concerned. That small but emphatic
turn of the body the instant before the club
starts to descend causes the implement to come
down on the same track as that which it occupied
when going up. It is sent out into much the
same position as that which it occupied at the top
of the swing for the cut mashie stroke. Round
it comes with quickening speed until it cuts right
across the ball. The position of the body is recovered at the moment of impact, and the follow-
through is as full and rhythmic, providing that
the stroke has been properly played, as for a plain
drive, although the club is travelling in a different
direction—across the line to the hole, in fact,
instead of on it.

I am aware that this explanation refutes the
assertion which I have previously made as to the
necessity of letting the club always lead, with
the body following. The intentional cut is the one

shot in which the body should lead at the top of
the swing and the arms move next. It is the
precedence of body movement that produces the
unintentional slice, similarly will it secure the intentional effect. The effort needs an abandonment
of most of the essentials of ordinary golf; you
do not even aim behind you at the beginning of
the downward swing. That turn at the hips sends
the club out slightly in front. It must be done
neatly and without a jerk, and it must be kept
strictly within limits. You do not want to make
a jump which will prevent you from obtaining a
perfect poise of the body for the moment of impact. The balance must be restored during the
second half of the downward swing, if I may so
describe that part which comes into being after
the arms have gone slightly forward. It must be
a small, smooth, and easily recoverable displace-
ment of the body. Then it will, I think, secure the
deliberate slice better than any other method. It
is, at any rate, the system on which I always
execute the shot.

Particularly careful should the player be not
to turn his right hand over as he strikes the ball.
If you turn the right hand over only a little, the
result must almost inevitably be a pull, and as you
are already aiming to the left of the line, the ball
will swing round to the on-side in a hair-raising
manner. I remember on one occasion in America
committing an error of this kind. It was in a
match against the best ball of two very good
golfers at Boston. I recollect it so well because,
after a lot of travelling, I did not feel a bit like
entering on a hard game. I opened a paper, and
almost the first item that caught my eye was a
paragraph headed:—" Vardon arrives: Confident
of winning and beating record."

I never in my life felt less like doing those

things. We duly reached the teeing ground. The first hole was a short one. The green could be reached with a cleek. Far away to the left (it looked too far off for anybody to get near to it) was a pond. I played, and pulled my ball what seemed to be miles off the course—plump into the middle of the pond. What the spectators could have thought just then of the man who was "confident of winning and beating record," as the paper had inconsiderately said of me, I have no idea. Perhaps, however, the incident roused me. At any rate, I really did play well after it, and accomplished what the imaginative writer had evidently expected me to do. But if you would like to know the worst shot I ever played, that start at Boston would be a good answer.

From the foregoing remarks it may be gathered that the way to impart intentional draw to the ball is to turn the right hand over at the instant of striking—or, at least, turn it half over. It is the easiest thing in the world to overdo the movement; that is why, in a high wind, the shot is so hazardous. If you turn the right hand over only a fraction of an inch too much, the effect of the excess is apt to be prodigious; the ball curls round like a boomerang, and tears across to the other side of the course, assisted by the wind. The stance is, to all intents and purposes, the exact antithesis of that for the slice. In the address, the ball should be just about opposite to the middle of the right foot. The left foot should be well forward so that the player finds himself distinctly in front of the ball and standing for a shot to the right of the line. Now, more than at any other time, is the occasion for remembering to hold tightly with the thumb and forefinger of the right hand. The face of the club must turn delicately on to the ball as the instrument comes down,

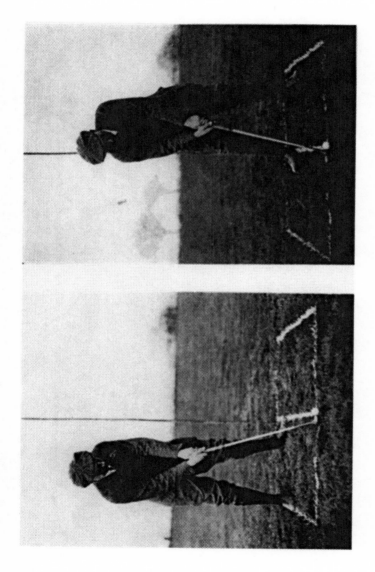

INTENTIONAL SLICING AND PULLING

Stance for the slice. The feet have moved completely behind the ball

Stance for the pull. The opposite of that for the slice. The feet have moved to the front of the ball

and if you grip a little tighter with the right hand than with the left, you have a considerable chance of securing this effect without worrying unduly about it. It is, perhaps, an instinct in the matter of the grip, combined with the correct stance, that makes a player what is called "a natural puller." This shot is much safer on a calm day than in a wind, because, in the absence of atmospheric disturbance, there is a considerable chance of finishing on the course even if the turn-over of the right hand be executed to excess.

Naturally on a tranquil day, it is not necessary to aim so far to the right as when a wind is ready to exert its influence, but the principles of the stroke hold good for all occasions. It is by a good deal the longest driving shot "on the market," and as it does not entail great risk when the elements are at peace, it is rapidly becoming an obsession. Good golfers and excellent fellows are becoming intoxicated with the passion for length, and they are playing all their shots with draw. Having got into the way of doing it, they cannot get out of it. They are mechanical pullers. That is where they are handicapped, for the shot is not often useful except for full drives. With this subject I have dealt, however, at the beginning of the book. Sufficient let it be if I suggest to the aspirant to fame that he should not neglect the other strokes in the game, strokes of inestimable importance, in his efforts to master this shot that gratifies the eminently human desire to make the ball go a very long way. Let him be as determined to practise the slice, the length of which shot can be judged with accuracy since it is nearly all carry, as the pull, which produces a flat carry and a long canter. He will be all the better for the diversity of his methods.

I suppose that, for the indifferent performer,

there is no experience more trying than that of playing a hole in the teeth of a strong wind. The ball never seems to go any distance, and it has an aggravating way of being caught in the gale and coming back towards its owner just when it might reasonably have rewarded his clean hit by travelling a bit farther than usual. He often discovers that a topped shot which goes straight serves him as well as a properly struck ball. That is because the former dodges the wind, but as topping is not the proper game, it is obviously his duty to keep the ball as low as possible while making sure of raising it from the ground. First of all the tee should be low. The stance should be forward—not quite so forward as for the push-shot, but with the hands the smallest distance conceivable in front of the ball during the address. That is the most important principle of the shot; for then, given a true swing, the club will come down on the ball in such a way as to keep it down throughout its flight. As the implement descends most of the weight should be transferred to the left leg, so that the body may go forward slightly with the club. Obviously the whole tendency of the stance and action is to beat the ball down, as it were, while hitting it so cleanly as to lift it from the tee. The iron shot against the wind should be a push-shot pure and simple. Nothing else is quite so good, for an adverse wind provides the ideal circumstances in which to make the most of the "push."

Golf down wind is a simple business, so long as you pay sufficient prospective attention to the hazards ahead. The drive is easy; the chief danger is that of getting into a bunker which is meant to catch a bad second shot. In the absence of such peril, tee high (but not so high as to introduce the possibility of hitting under the ball), stand rather behind the ball, swing truly, and at the time of impact throw most of the weight on to the right leg so as to lift the ball into the air, and give it the full benefit of the wind. In approaching, it is not bad to remember what I have already written as to the preferableness, on hard ground, of hugging the bunkers on the wings at the risk of making their acquaintance. This, however, must be left to the player's judgment, and to the situation that is offered on the other side of the green, whither the ball may make its ungovernable way.

Personally, the worst wind I ever experienced was that which prevailed during the open championship at Hoylake in 1907, when Arnaud Massy plugged his way so gallantly to victory. It was terrific. The fourth hole, a short one, which can often be played with a mashie, required a full driver shot, and even that had to be kept low in order to escape the full force of the gale that was raging overhead. I like Hoylake, and one of the few faults I have ever seen in it was the bank which had been raised for that occasion a few yards in front of the fourth teeing ground. In order to reach the green, it was necessary to drive very low, and a lot of men who played the only shot for the occasion (Mr John Ball, I believe, among the number) were caught by that bank about five yards in front of the place from which the ball had started. One player had a most exciting experience; he went from the bank into the shelter hard by, and dodged all round the teeing ground until at length he reached the green in, I think, 7, and holed out in 9.

At the sixth hole, it was impossible to get even up to the corner of the garden with the drive. Massy played some great golf during that trying week.

The next worst wind I remember was that which prevailed during the tournament at Newcastle, Co. Down, in 1898. There was rain, too, in bucketfuls. I know that, in the qualifying competition, we positively ran round; those who did not sprint round the links ran into the club-house. Many players retired at the third hole, and the course was bestrewn with the remains of umbrellas. On the night before the final, in which I met Taylor, I asked the attendant at the place in which I was staying to see that my golf boots were dry by the morning. He saw to it most effectually. I do not know whether he put them on the fire or in the oven; at any rate, as I made my first tee-shot in the morning, they both split right across the sole. The best game I ever played in my life with the gutta-percha ball was played in that ruined foot-gear. I have since wondered in times of adversity whether it would be a good thing to split my boots.

The wind is a fine educator; I recommend the golfer to lose no opportunity to coquet with it. For the present, however, he must have had enough of it. I only hope that he has not been involved in it so long as to leave him tired and struggling for his breath.

Stance for a drive against the wind, the hands are very slightly in front of the ball

IN THE WIND

A drive down wind. The body is more behind the ball than for an ordinary shot

CHAPTER XII

NUMEROUS and varied are the ills to which the golfing flesh is heir. Fortunately it is nearly always possible for an experienced player to diagnose with accuracy the disease of stance or swing which is causing distress to a fellow-golfer, point out to him the character of his burden, and suggest a cure. In that respect, golf is different from most other outdoor games. The ball is struck from a stationary position; consequently, cause is as clearly defined as effect to the person who has made a deep study of the shots.

Occasionally, in the case of an ordinary good player who is temporarily harassed by a slight deviation from the correct method, the secret of the trouble is hard to fathom. I know of one excellent golfer who, in a time of adversity, called together quite a large party of championship winners in order that they might examine his methods, confer as to the nature of his affliction, and prescribe. After a little while they discovered the origin of the disease, and effected a cure. The discussion that proceeded while the patient displayed his swing was solemn in the extreme; it was like a meeting of specialists at a critical point in a grave illness. Still, it had good results. Naturally, in the case of an indifferent player, diagnosis is easier, because the faults are generally more pronounced. My object in this chapter is to deal with affections that often visit themselves upon the moderate golfer, to explain the cause of such distressing phenomena, and to indicate how they may be eradicated. I do not propose to launch out, like a quack doctor, with the remark that I have a cure for every complaint. Much must be left to the heedfulness and diligence of the patient himself. Moreover, there are some cases so terribly complicated (the stance, the swing, and everything else are wrong), that there is little hope for the victim unless he decides to forget his present methods, and start the game over again in the proper way. He must make a new golfer of himself. An instance of this kind comes to my mind. The victim of chronic incorrectness whom I have in view is one of the best-hearted men I know, and I must confess that he derives boundless enjoyment from the pursuit of the pastime in his own peculiar way; but his style is really enough to make the hair of an instructor stand on end.

In some extraordinary manner he hits the ball with the top of the club-head—that is to say, on that part where the name is engraved. This is not merely an occasional eccentricity; he does the same thing with nearly every shot he plays, even through the green. He wears the name off the wood in next to no time. He cannot use iron clubs because the surface at the top of the head is not sufficiently big to enable him to hit the ball. Rumour says that he has never been known to strike with the face. To hear him call for a spoon when he is right under a hedge is

almost paralyzing. I once followed his fortunes
for about ten minutes on a certain course. Starting from the fourth tee, he directed the ball by
a series of zig-zag movements on to a green
of the homeward half. Having dropped his ball
at the side, he proceeded to scoop it on to yet
another green in the last nine holes. He was
still playing to the fourth. From his new base
of operations, he got into a pond which was supposed to be a hazard for another hole which he
had yet to tackle. Ultimately he reached the
fourth green after having worked his way completely round it. The man who is so philosophic
as to be able to thoroughly enjoy the game even
when he plays it very badly is an enviable soul.
I do, indeed, covet his happy disposition. The
great majority of golfers, however, earnestly
desire to execute the shots properly, and
when a person finds that he is doing nearly
everything wrongly, I can but recommend him to
place himself in the hands of a capable coach, and
learn whether his only remedy is the desperate one
of retracing his footsteps to the place from which
he started, and beginning his career as a golfer
in an amended manner.

Let us consider, however, the case of the player
who is in possession of the right ideas, but who
is suffering tribulation on account of a temporary
incapacity to put those ideas into operation. He
should look first to ascertain that he is gripping
properly. He may have fallen unwittingly into
the habit of placing one hand or the other too
far under the shaft, or he may have gone to the
opposite extreme, which is equally bad. Whether
the golfer effects the overlapping grip or the
older two-V grip, in which the hands touch but
do not overlap, it is important to see that the
knuckles are neither under nor over the shaft

K

of the club. As nearly as makes no difference, the knuckles of the left hand should be facing the line of play, while those of the right hand should be pointing in the other direction. I am writing of course, of right-handed golf. In no circumstances should the knuckles of either hand be looking down at the turf or up at the sky.

A frequent cause of disaster, especially with iron clubs, is failure to ground the implement in a reasonable manner behind the ball. The proper way is the easiest; that, perhaps, is why so many thousands of people do not take advantage of it. In golf, as in other affairs of life, humanity has a knack of making things difficult for itself. There is no surer means of learning how far to stand from the ball than the simple expedient of seeing that the whole length of the club's sole, from toe to heel, is resting on the turf when the club is grounded. Yet there are countless players who take up their stance and perform the ceremony of the address with the toe of the cleek, iron, or mashie cocked into the air. Having occupied a position a goodly distance from the ball for the driver shot, they appear to be afraid of drawing appreciably closer when they have to select one of the shorter clubs. So far as one can judge, they fear that they may get so near as to be unable to swing freely. They ought to be considerably closer for the iron or the mashie than for the driver. They may rest assured that if they have space sufficient in which to swing back, they will have just as much room in which to come down again. There is such a fault as getting too close to the ball, but it is a blight which affects only one player for every fifty golfers who do not stand near enough for their iron shots. They reach forward in a strained manner—a process which in itself compels them to stoop unduly—with the result that they have very little chance of either pivoting properly or grazing the turf with the length of the club's sole as they execute the stroke. It is easy to fall into the habit of stretching the arms too much in the address in order to reach the ball; it is equally easy to avoid this straining by closing in a little on the ball. Therefore, let the player who is in the throes of purgatory satisfy himself that he is gripping properly, and soling the club properly.

The right stance comes readily to the golfer once he knows the game, but it does not present itself without being sought. It is seldom a gift, and it can rarely be left to look entirely after itself. It has to be studied, and the knowledge acquired during the course of education has to be exercised for every shot. Some players stand with their feet so far apart, and others with their feet so close together, that they cannot possibly distribute their weight evenly. Stance is a matter of great importance, and I recommend the aspirant to success to pay the closest attention to it.

Amongst beginners, the most common fault is topping. That is curious, because, to the person who has come to be capable of playing a good game, intentional topping is one of the most difficult feats in the realm of golf. As it is valueless, nobody endeavours to cultivate it, but, in capricious moments, I have tried to accomplish it consistently, and have concluded the trials in a state of wonderment at the beginner's capacity for it. I am saying this in no spirit of exaltation, and with no desire to mock the victim of an attack of unintentional topping; I am merely trying to induce him to believe that it is the

easiest disease in the world to expel from
the system for the simple reason that it is the
hardest to retain. There is very little space at
which to hit in order to come down on top of a
ball. That the novice should repeatedly light on
that small area is one of the mysteries of the
game.

Topping is nearly always caused by either
straightening the body, and therefore lifting the
head at the instant of impact, or hugging the arms
up towards the chest as the club nears the
ball. Swaying to the right and failing to recover
during the downward swing will also promote
topping, but the same fault will produce nearly
every other affliction to which the golfing race
is susceptible, so that its ravages cannot be discussed under this heading alone. What often
happens is that the player takes the club back
properly and still tops—through either lifting his
head or jerking his arms up as the club meets
the ball. In the latter case, he has usually been
attacked by a sudden apprehension that there is
no room for the implement to go through to
the finish of the stroke. He thinks that he is
going to hit the ground a long way behind the
ball, and makes a desperate effort to put things
right. The almost inevitable issue is a topped
shot. If, having addressed the ball, he will focus
his attention on the swing, he need have little
fear as to the club finding all the space that it
wants for its work. It is when he tries to alter
its course that he comes to grief. Lifting the
head may be due to anxiety to see the result
of the stroke, or to an involuntary movement
for which the player cannot account. That is to
say, he perhaps straightens his posture while
still keeping his eye fixed on the spot which the
ball is leaving. He may not even know that his

body (and with it his head) has risen an inch or so. Assiduous practice alone will master this fault, and I would recommend the unhappy victim to engage in the task in company with that device which helped so much to make Colonel Quill a scratch player at the age of fifty-six. It is surprising how the thing induces you to keep your head down. It is the best cure for topping that I know.

Slicing is the most unprofitable vice in the game. A crooked shot that goes a considerable distance is not wholly awful; there is a silver lining to the cloud, to which the player draws attention by remarking to his opponent:—" It went a deuce of a long way, anyhow." The worst of the sliced ball is that it seldom travels very far. As a rule it is caused by swaying the body to the right during the upward swing (that is to say, not turning at the hips), or by perpetrating at the top of the swing, when the hips have screwed up properly, the common error of beginning to unwind at the hips before starting the club on its return journey. Assuming that the golfer knows how to swing, this premature movement of the body is nearly always the cause of slicing. It results in the arms being thrown forward, whereupon the face of the instrument cuts across the ball and produces the slice. The remedy is to determine that the club-head shall always lead, and to aim at the beginning of the downward swing at a point slightly behind the player. It is a good tip to take up a position close to a tree (although not sufficiently near to hit it) so that the timber is to the right of you and a few inches in the rear of the line which you are occupying. Then, turning the hips correctly to the top of the swing, try to imagine that you want to hit that tree as the club comes down.

As previously explained, it is necessary for an intentional slice to give the body a slight turn before the start of the downward swing (at least, that is how I secure the effect); in just the same way is the slice provoked when you are not standing for it, and do not want it. When playing for a straight shot, the club should begin to descend before the body changes from its top-of-the-swing position, save in one respect. As the club starts to return, the left hip may be pushed slightly towards the hole—not unscrewed, but urged an inch or two sideways so as to facilitate the unwinding of the frame which follows immediately. For the rest, the arms should follow the club as it comes down, and the body should follow the arms as they come round. If you aim behind at the outset, the body will not often turn first.

Pulling is a curious phase of the game. In certain circumstances a little of it is excellent because it goes such a long way, or rather makes the ball go such a long way. The veriest trifle more than the desired quantum of pull, however, often spells disaster. Ten or twelve years ago, the natural slicer was more common than the natural puller; nowadays, the latter predominates, and, indeed, almost fills the golfing universe. As a consequence, the ugly hook which sends the ball off the course to the left is perhaps the most frequent of faults; for, in the manner of its execution, it is not greatly different from the skilful pull. It is often caused by a failure to turn the left wrist at the beginning of the upward swing, so that the knuckles are visible, if you turn your head to look for them, instead of being so far over the club as to be out of sight. Take an iron club three-quarters of the way up; stop in the

IN THE BEGINNING

The wrong back swing.   The left wrist has not turned sufficiently, and therefore the club face has not turned away from the ball

IN THE BEGINNING
The correct up-swing

position thus obtained, and then examine your
left hand. If it is so turned away from you that
you can see only one or two of the knuckles, it is
wrong. The lot ought to be visible because the
left wrist ought to be under the shaft—not pointing skywards.

Another provocation of the pull is the fault
of holding tighter with one hand than the
other, and a third is turning the right hand over
at the moment of impact. The first and last of
these causes are practically synonymous. As
the implement goes back the face of it should be
turning away from the ball, so that it may resume
only at the instant of hitting the position which
it occupied when it was grounded behind the ball.
If you do not turn the club-face away by gently
screwing the left wrist at the start, the chances
are that the right hand will have control coming
down, and be in the same position as if that hand
had been turned over quickly at the critical
moment. Holding tighter with one hand than
the other produces much the same effect. There
are people who say that you should grip
tighter with the left hand than with the right.
Personally, I think there ought to be no distinction. The tight hold with left hand is apt
to drag the right hand over, and the result is a pull. I am sure all good golfers
grip as firmly with one hand as with the other.
I know that for an ordinary swing my own
right hand is no more relaxed than the left at
any stage of the movement. If the left hand were
really the master hand, if one hand did all the
hard work and the other merely acted as a guide,
surely it would be possible, with a true swing, to
drive as far with one hand as with two. I have
tried single-handed driving. I have hit the ball
correctly and made it go straight, and have never

succeeded in inducing it to travel anything like so far as with two hands. The one helps as much as the other to secure distance; of that I am certain after submitting the idea of a " master hand " to exhaustive trials. In no circumstances should the right hand be the predominant partner. By his wooden clubs shall ye know what may be called " the right-hand hitter." He wears away the wood at the back of the sole, and reaches the inset of lead in a very short time. That is because he is constantly coming down on the back of the sole. Neither is it, however, correct to be a " left-hand hitter," that is to say, to make the left do most of the work. I feel convinced that every first-class player uses his two hands without giving them distinctive duties to perform. Too much left is as bad as too much right; either is apt to produce the hooked shot. The simplest remedy for this error is to make sure of turning the face of the club away from the ball at the beginning of the upward swing so that the tendency of the right to assume command may be checked. When that turn of the left wrist has been completed early in the swing, the golfer should not be conscious that one hand is trying to do more than the other.

In all these matters, it is essential to remember to screw your hips properly and keep your head steady. Very many golfers do everything correctly when taking the club to the top of the swing, and cut off a segment, so to speak, in coming down. They throw their arms forward immediately; they miss that section just behind them—the section which they had to form in order to get the club up after having turned the left wrist inwards. Instead of following the same track for the return journey, they take a short cut across the corner. Out goes the club, and then anything may happen. There must be no sudden movement of this description. If in the middle of the task of winding up a clock you were to give the key a sudden and desperately violent twist, you would very likely realize in the course of a minute or so that the works had gone wrong. So will the golf swing go wrong if you try to come down by making a quick dash across the track which the club occupied in its upward course. This throwing out of the arms is a frequent cause of distress in connexion with iron shots. Players imagine that they are farther from the ball than is actually the case. The idea seizes them at the top of the swing, they reach forward directly they start to come down in order to make sure of getting to the ball, and the whole operation is ruined. In the case of a mashie stroke, the face of the club knocks the ball on to the socket and sends it to perdition. The best cure for socketting is to determine that the left arm shall graze the coat both going up and coming down. If the left arm can be induced to caress the jacket all the way, the right arm cannot stray, and the action is correct.

Schlaffing is caused by throwing the weight on to the right leg at the moment of hitting, and therefore dropping the right shoulder too quickly. The right shoulder has to come down in order to produce the proper effect, but it must not drop suddenly.

There are some players who, while they nearly always strike the ball accurately and make it travel in a straight line, never succeed in driving far. The reason is that they are not making sufficient use of their arms. They are executing the stroke purely by the twist of the body, and not putting their arms into it. It is the fact that the arms have to be used in order to obtain distance that

makes the golfing swing partly a hit. The idea
of " sweeping the ball off the tee " is very well
in its way, but the arms, kept in decorous
position by the trueness of the swing, have
to hit, or the shot will be of very modest
length.

I think that we have considered most of the
common ailments of the golfer, but there are a
few points of a general character that may be
mentioned before we leave the sick-chamber. In
the first place, the player who aspires to real
success should never capitulate to the idea of trying to cure a slice that is habitual by playing for a
pull, or vice versa. At first blush, such a scheme
may seem to have much to recommend it, but if
he decide to adopt it, he will be reduced, sooner
or later, to a state of despair. He will never
know quite where he is going; he will be all hope
and fear. As a rule, the corrective influence will
be either too weak or too strong; if it be too
strong he will find himself endeavouring to
remedy his new fault by cultivating the action
which he set out to eradicate. I know many
golfers who have practised this plan of existing on antidotes, but I have never met one
who has made a success of the conspiracy.
Another important point is to make sure that
you really are slicing or pulling before you attempt
to cure the assumed defect. You may be standing in such a way that a straight shot is sure to
go to either the left or the right of the fairway.
During the address, the face of the club should
be square to the line which you propose to follow.
And beware of altering your intentions at the top
of the swing. I must confess that this is a counsel
of perfection up to which I do not always act in
my own golf. It is one of the trials of the game
that, just before the club starts to come down,

the player suddenly conceives a fancy for executing the shot in a manner quite different from that which had fixed itself in his mind during the upward swing. Such a change is not often for the best.

CHAPTER XIII

NEXT to the joy of playing a round there is no
more engaging occupation for the keen
habitué of the links than that of studying the
methods of acknowledged masters of the game.
Golf can be learnt by example as well as by precept, and I am certain that by watching, thinking
and practising, it is possible for anybody to go
on adding to his store of knowledge and degree
of efficiency till the end of his playing days, or,
at any rate, till the finish of those days which
precede the development of a rigid body and stiff
knees. The crowd at a golf match consists
chiefly of enthusiasts who want to see causes as
well as effects. The latter are summed up in the
result, but I suppose that, to most of the onlookers, the issue is a matter of little importance.
What they are anxious to learn is how the
players secure the result. It is the best kind of
curiosity in the world, because it shows that the
great majority of people regard the game in the
proper light; that is to say, they realize its scientific beauties. They desire to observe not only
whether the ball has been hit on to the green, but
how the performer has gone about the task of
landing it there. The man who is taking part in

an exhibition match appreciates to the full the penetrative mind of the " gallery," and the occasional captious critic who insinuates that professionals do not worry their head very much when participating in exhibition games is hopelessly mistaken and grievously unjust. Nobody could play golf well unless he tried hard to do so, and professionals simply have to play well. There is no danger of golf ever being regarded as an entertainment at the expense of its place in the world as an active recreation; consequently, one may reasonably suggest to all aspirants to success that they should seize every opportunity of examining the methods of good players. This particular pursuit is already popular, and its growth cannot fail to be profitable to the standard of the game. It is pleasant, too, for the exhibitor to feel that the followers are closely observant of his methods. From time to time, I have had curious questions put to me during the progress of rounds as to the way in which this or that shot has been executed, and I am sure that I have always been sensible of the compliments conveyed by such manifestations of interest.

Edward Ray is a man whom I like to watch on the links. He defies so many of the accepted principles of the game; he is so very nearly a complete set of laws unto himself. He sways appreciably, and heaves at the ball. He is a master of the knack of recovering the right position at the moment of impact after having moved his head and body during the backward swing in a degree that would spell disaster to almost anybody else. He is the brilliant exception to a safe rule. As he brings the club down, you feel that he is either going to make an extraordinarily good shot or an extraordinarily bad one. He is getting into the proper position all the while; it is just a question as to whether he will be able to resume the even distribution of his weight at the instant of hitting. His terrific lunge almost brings your heart into your mouth lest he should miss the shot. You wonder where on earth the ball will go in the event of such a catastrophe. Then you look up, and see the article sailing down the middle of the course. At the psychological moment he has done everything correctly. Ray has his own way of playing golf, and it is fine to see because of its individuality. His drives and his cleek shots, with their great length of carry, are among the best things in the game.

Probably, however, his favourite shot is the long approach which he plays with his niblick. He is a marvel at it. Here, perhaps, you are cogitating as to the manner in which you shall get up with a straight-faced iron, when you suddenly see Ray thump his ball to the hole-side with a niblick. He told me that, during the open championship which he won at Muirfield, he chose that club for his second shot to the tenth hole. He was in the rough to the right, and the second shot of something over 100 yards had to be nearly all carry so as to clear the big sandhill. And he did this with a niblick!

Given the chance, I like nothing better than the diversion of watching the play of other people. I wish I had seen more of the golf of the leading amateurs; not having had chances of studying them frequently, perhaps I ought not to criticise their methods. When one is engaged in a round honoured by the presence of a large "gallery," there is not always much opportunity of distinguishing the manner in which the opponent sets about his task. It is exceedingly useful to observe what he does, and what reward he reaps; especially is this the case on clay courses, where one cannot always be sure as to the pace and other peculiarities of the ground, and where, therefore, the advantage of compelling the other man to play the " odd " is more than ordinarily useful. During a tournament or exhibition match, however, a professional is apt to be enveloped by the onlookers directly he has accomplished his shot. He finds himself in a whirling, eddying crowd, and before he has struggled clear of it and replied to questions as to how he likes the links, and whether he has ever played at Pushem-along-the-mire, his rival has reached the green, and the educative phrase of the process has been lost on the man who now has to supply the " like." For that reason, I know less than I would like to know about the methods of several very fine players whom I have had few chances of watching, but who have heaped discomfiture upon my head. Still, there are well-known golfers with whom I have been in more or less constant contact for many years, and whose modes of operation I have had chances of conning in the course of some hundreds of meetings. For instance, I have come to the conclusion that I enjoy nothing more than the sight of Braid getting out of the rough. The choice may not indicate a Christian spirit, but the best—or worst—of Braid in the rough is that it generally means no punishment at all to him. It is a real treat to watch him playing a shot in an extremely difficult position. He has no equal at it. The only place in which he is beaten is the place in which he has no room to swing his club. Give him just enough space to raise the implement and he will recover from anything. I hope it will be understood that I wish Braid nothing but good; but I really would like to see him more often in the rough—his getting out of it is such a thrilling spectacle. The trouble may be gorse or rank grass, or rocks or a railway track; as he takes the club up you realize that something will have to go, and that the ball will go with it. He brings his niblick down with terrific power; there is nothing like it in the rest of golf. He plays a perfect shot in a bunker. I remember he remarked on one occasion that he did not mind being photographed; but that he wished that the pictures were not so monotonous in depicting him in difficulties. "People will think I am always in bunkers," was the neat way in which he summed up the situation. I know from long experience that Braid is very seldom in trouble. His skill in avoiding it has robbed the golfing world of many magnificent strokes that he would otherwise have executed in getting out of it.

If you want to see the push-shot played to perfection, there is nobody better to watch than Braid. Addressing the ball with his hands a little in front of it, he takes the club back in a more upright manner than for the ordinary stroke. Then at the moment of impact, his arms lengthen (or at any rate straighten) and he pushes them through as he gives the object a mighty thump. As I have previously remarked, I would recommend everybody who has reached the stage of ordinary proficiency to practise this push-shot. The proper accomplishment of it affords more gratification than anything else in the game. Indeed, I venture to say that nobody knows how joyous a pursuit is golf until he learns the push-shot. To loft a ball into the air is a soulless operation by comparison with the feat of making it travel for a considerable distance in one plane. Personally, I play nearly all my strokes with iron clubs in this way; it is the safest as well as the most pleasurable manner. Whether the shot is well named I do not know. It is a mixture of swing, hit, and push, with the last-named influence introduced at the moment of striking so that the arms push through the ball, and, thus extended, finish in such a way that the right forearm is pointing up towards the sky. Its nomenclature might be improved, but as the push-shot we know it. And it is the best shot in golf.

J. H. Taylor is a great player. I like his full iron shots up to the hole quite as much as his mashie shots, for which he is so justly famed. His cut stroke with the mashie is a picture; he seems to be born to execute it in the ideal manner. You will notice that, for all his shots, he stands with the face of the club turned slightly away from the ball. I presume that he always aims a trifle to the left of the pin, and cuts the ball. That being his natural method, his excellence at the cut mashie stroke is understandable. Taylor can always be watched with advantage; his swing is beautifully under control, and he hits the ball with that nip —that element of resolution—which counts for so much in the execution of a shot. For the man who has developed an inclination to falter and check the pace of the club before reaching the ball I would recommend a survey of Taylor playing a round. He is never caught trying to coax his rubber-core; he gives it a forceful blow every time. That is the only way to make it fulfil one's requirements.

Another very fine mashie player is Arnaud Massy, but he secures his effect in a fashion different from that adopted by any other prominent golfer whom I have ever seen. He introduces an enormous amount of "stop" into his lofted shots, and obtains the influence by means of a swing which is peculiar to himself. At the top of the swing, he gives the club a flourish which sends it over his head. Then he brings it back

L

again, and down in the same track as that which it occupied when going up.

Alexander Herd is a master of the spoon. Whenever you hear him call for that club, you can rest assured (or if you happen to be his opponent you can becalm yourself with resignation) that he is going to reach the green. He gets a lot of cut on to his spoon shot, and makes it drop right up by the hole. He swings for it in just the same way as for the cleek, but gives his body a slight turn at the hips before the club starts to come down, and so obtains the effect of the slice. George Duncan is another great spoon player; indeed, I have seen him use the implement on many occasions in a manner which I do not think anybody else could have attained. In any case, if it were a matter of a contest amongst professionals for supremacy with the spoon, Duncan's one formidable rival would be, I believe, Herd. Both men employ "cut," which is an invaluable and necessary action with this club, and they introduce the influence very cleverly. When Duncan and I played Braid and Sherlock in a foursome at Stoke Poges a few years ago, my partner must have grown somewhat weary after a while of hearing me ask him to take his spoon. Duncan has a perfect swing, but he is so extraordinarily quick that it is very hard to tell how he executes his shots. The ball is on the ground and he is addressing it; a moment later, while you are still waiting to study his movements, the ball is hurtling through the air, and he is off for the next stroke. He is by far the most rapid golfer I have ever seen. He reminds me of the story of a professional who was giving a lesson to a gentleman of ebullient temperament. The latter had been supplied with the usual preliminary hints, including the "Slow back" maxim; he did not appear

to be greatly impressed by any of them. He took
his driver back in whirlwind fashion; missed the
globe, and nearly tumbled over. " You must take
the club up much more slowly than that," said the
instructor. " Rot ! " was the reply. The student
made another attempt; his action was still that of
a "backmarker in a forked lightning congress."
Again the professional protested. " Stand away !
Stand away ! " screamed the beginner, a ferocious
gleam in his eye, " I've been quick all my life,
and I'm not going slowly at this darned game."
That is a sample of the trials that enter into the
life of a golf professional. He tries to do his
work conscientiously; and sometimes has enormous difficulty in inducing the pupil to assist
himself.

There are many other splendid players, whose
methods I fain would have the opportunity of
studying more closely. We can learn at golf till
the end of life, and a keen observance of the styles
of skilful performers often generates inspiration
and encouragement. There is Tom Ball, with that
gloriously confident manner of putting, and
peculiarity of appearing to hit the ball off the toe
of the putter. He is a monumental tribute, too,
to the importance of keeping the eye on the ball;
even when the latter object is in the hole after he
has played a putt of five or six feet, his eye has not
moved. There is Fred Robson, with his beautiful
brassie shots; there is James Sherlock, with his
charmingly simple system of obtaining great
length by means of an apparently gentle tap. I
think he must talk to the ball, and coax it into a
friendly state. I am sure that he is a master of the
low-flying shot with pull, executed by the half-
turn of the right hand. If you would know that
shot, watch Sherlock. An excellent player of
iron shots is my brother Tom. I very much like

watching him execute his half-cleeks up to the hole.

In conclusion, I would ask you to remember that the professional gives of his best when he plays golf. The game is not so easy to him that he can play it well without trying to do so. I am certain that it is not easy to anybody. One dare not be careless at golf. The very constitution of the pastime declines to tolerate heedlessness. If you are following a professional match, you may depend upon it that the players are striving their utmost to produce perfect effects. The people who talk about the accomplishment of the strokes as a mere formality to the men who take part in exhibition games do not appreciate the science of golf in its fullness. It is never a formality. The best day's golf that I ever played with the rubber-cored ball was in an exhibition match. By "best" I am referring to the match in which my game gave me the greatest amount of personal satisfaction, and which I could not have played better in a heavenly sort of dream. Whenever I start to think about my golfing life, or whenever a few of us talk of our experiences, the recollection of this event comes to me instantly.

The occasion was a contest with Tom Williamson on a nine-holes course at Radcliffe-on-Trent. The club had offered a very fine cup for the winner, and Williamson and I were as keen as mustard on winning it. We both saw it overnight, and I am certain that each of us had no other ambition at the time than to capture that trophy. I felt in just the right mood in the morning, and I played as I had never played before, and have never played since, with the rubber-core. It was a good course, with a proper proportion of holes that required two shots. I did the nine holes in scores of 31, 32, and 31, and won by 11 up and 9 to play.

Williamson hardly made a mistake, but I kept on laying my approaches within holing distance. He would get on to the green in two, and lay his long putt stone dead, and then I would get down with the like. I remember that in the afternoon I had three 2's, one of them at the ninth, which was obtained by holing a mashie shot that finished the match. Williamson's father was as excited as any of us about the event, and he really was glum when the affair ended so early. A friend of his, who had hastened to the course to see what he could of the match, came up just as we finished, and inquired anxiously how the game stood. "Oh," said Williamson, senior, "it's been a terrible fiasco. Only one man turned up to play, and he wasn't Tom."

I have mentioned this not in any spirit of self-glorification, but to show that professionals are earnest triers in exhibition games. Such events not infrequently find the player in better form than during a championship.

CHAPTER XIV

CLAY is, I daresay, essential to the stability of the land—as land—and we have enough of it in all conscience in this country. There are more clayey golf courses than of any other denomination of soil, and their prevalence means that the game of golf is not quite the same at all seasons of the year. It is one of the failings of the moderate player, who gives little thought to details, that he seldom considers the question of altering his methods so as to accommodate himself to varying conditions. On seaside and dry inland greens, no change of system is required. So long as the golfer keeps to the fairway, the ball generally sits up for him with some nobleness of bearing, and the stroke can be executed in much the same manner in the winter as in the summer. The habitué of a clayey course leads a much more diverting life. If he would maintain the standard of his game throughout the twelve months, he must learn several shots at the beginning of the dank days which he will need to forget upon the advent of the dry period; he must have his summer methods and his winter methods. He must know just when to exercise either, but that need not cause him much trouble, since it takes him little time to tell whether he has a good lie or a bad one through the green. At least, it does not usually take him long to tell everybody within hail when he has a bad lie.

Naturally, it is in the play through the green that the principal differences arise. The tee shot is the tee shot all the world over, and in every period of the year; but on a clayey course the second shot in November is often a proposition totally unlike that which presents itself in August. Every golfer appreciates and allows for the difference in the run of the ball; that is an elementary matter which speaks for itself. What very many players do not realize is the necessity of amending their principles in several important respects when the courses become heavy. They follow the methods which perhaps proved highly profitable during the summer, and generally arrive at the conclusion that winter golf is an abomination, tolerable only because it is better than no golf at all. I must confess that it is not always a thing of beauty or a joy for even a day, and I envy the people who always play on dry greens. By taking into account, however, the altered circumstances, it is possible to obtain many good rounds on miry turf. The point to remember is not to endeavour in the ordinary way to accomplish the same shots through the green as one would attempt in the summer. It is because so many people try to do this that they feel discontented about their November to March golf.

It is no use, for instance, "pecking" at the ball, as one can do in dry conditions. So far as I have been able to observe, the great majority of golfers make the mistake, on heavy soil, of trying to take the ball cleanly. They usually bungle the stroke for the simple reason that the ground has a sufficiently tenacious hold of the object to prevent it from rising sharply when the club comes

into contact with it. After the driver (and before
the putter) the most valuable implement during
the winter is a fairly powerful mid-iron, and the
game to play with it on soft soil is to aim well
behind the ball and take a little turf. Often that
is the only way to secure anything like a shot,
and while our hearts may weep for the excavations
which we are perpetrating, we can at least retrieve
the divots and repair the earth which we have so
sadly maltreated. At a long hole, where it is
clearly impossible to reach the green in two
strokes, the safest game is usually to play a drive
and two strokes with the mid-iron or a nicely
lofted cleek.

I like the brassie, but it is not built for frequent
use in the mud. Where there are a fair number of
long holes, and its frequent employment seems
almost essential, it is a good idea to have two
clubs of the kind—one with a little loft on it
and the other with a distinct loft. The latter will
often prove valuable. A spoon, indeed, is an
exceedingly handy tool for winter golf. At no
time are its virtues more apparent than during the
wet season. Unless one has a fancy for it, there
is no particular reason for bringing it into
frequent play during the dry weather, but it is
often a stroke saver on heavy ground. It gets
under the ball, and that is everything in such
circumstances.

It is one of the misfortunes of the people who
play on muddy courses that they lose touch with
that interesting stroke—the cut shot with the
mashie. It cannot be accomplished on treacherous
turf. If you try to make the ball bite on the club,
you will merely dig the latter into the ground,
with consequent disaster. The niblick is sometimes a good club for approaching from a heavy
lie. It cuts into the turf, and if you play it with

sufficient strength to raise a divot and the ball
with it, the club will serve the purpose admirably.
On the whole, however, the mashie is the best
implement for approaches of moderate length, and
the soundest hint that one can give in connexion
with it is a warning not to try to do anything
particularly clever with it on sodden ground. A
plain lofting stroke of the right length is all that
can be attempted with safety. So that the winter
is a leveller of golfers so far as concerns the art
of approaching; there is no scope for executing
the more advanced shots, which ought to be a
satisfactory state of affairs for the multitude of
long-handicap players.

I suppose that, in time, there will be very few
wet winter courses. At present there are plenty,
but with the continued development of the game
in the scheme of the nation's recreation, the work
of draining is becoming better and better understood. What is equally important, the question
of money seldom, nowadays, presents a stumbling
block. Fifteen years ago, most of the greens
round London were little better during the wet
season than quagmires. Fishermen's waders
would have been, perhaps, the most sensible foot-
gear. The player squelched his way through the
swamps, scattering mud-showers with nearly every
shot that he executed through the green, and yet
finding a deal of enjoyment in his game. During
recent years the improvements have been wonderful. Take, for instance, the course with which
I have the honour of being associated—South
Herts, situated at Totteridge. It used to be as
damp as many another with a clayey soil. What
was very puzzling, the draining operations which
had been carried out failed in the first instance
to produce satisfactory results. So we over-
hauled the system of drainage, and discovered

that it offered a reasonable explanation of its inefficiency. In some cases, the pipes came to an end without being connected with any ditch or other natural channel for carrying off superfluous water. They followed devious routes, and stopped suddenly as though the designer had gone on planting them till his stock was exhausted, and then proceeded home with the conviction that he had done his best. There was nowhere for the water to empty itself, and so, for a time, we were distinctly on the wet side. We set about the work again, and laid down some 30,000 new pipes. The reward of that enterprise has been great. It has afforded ample proof of the possibilities of inducing a clay course to remain decently dry during the winter months.

CHAPTER XV

THE GAME ABROAD

GOLF has done wonders since it found its way out of Scotland, and, in connexion with its development, nothing has been more remarkable than its progress abroad. When, just over twenty years ago, I left Jersey and came to England to take up the game as a profession, it was beginning to obtain its grip on the affections of the English people. Outside the limits of the United Kingdom it occupied an exceedingly humble position. Even in this country players were not so numerous as one might have wished, and the professional had many opportunities of practising in splendid isolation. Such studying of all the points of the pastime doubtless did him a lot of good (it certainly helped me, for I spent nearly all my spare hours in learning new shots) but, at the time, it was not a particularly lucrative pursuit, and it required a deal of enthusiasm, since it seemed to be a matter of trying to secure a state of perfection in a department of life that interested comparatively few people.

It is a lucky circumstance to have lived through this crowded period which has seen golf rise from obscurity to a position among the world's great games. To recall its limited degree of importance

in the days of a quarter of a century ago, and
to turn from those memories to a conception
of its present magnitude, is a trial in contrasts
that almost numbs the brain. The difference is
so great as to be indescribable. And it is a
fine thing to know that golf is now the possession
of the universe, and not the hobby of one race.

I have played in the United States, France,
Germany, Belgium, Switzerland, and other
countries. Everywhere the enthusiasm of the
natives has been unmistakable. As an example
of zeal, I can imagine nothing better than an
incident that came under my notice at Le Touquet
three years ago. Two Frenchmen arrived to engage in a match. They found the course covered
with snow to the depth of several inches. They
were informed that golf was out of the
question, and so, indeed, the several British
golfers staying at the hotel had decided
finally and irrevocably. But the Frenchmen were
not to be deterred. They obtained some snow-
shoes, went out and played, and declared at the
finish that they had enjoyed the round immensely.
France is, I think, destined to be a great golfing
country. Every year sees an increase in the
number of players, and the clubs around Paris
are now recruited principally from French people,
whereas, a few years ago, they were supported
almost entirely by British and American residents
and visitors.

How vastly the standard of golf has improved
in the United States since I was there in 1900
it is easy to tell from the form of several American
amateurs, such as Mr W. J. Travis, Mr J. D.
Travers, Mr E. M. Byers, Mr C. Evans, and Mr
F. Herrshoff, who have visited this country during the past nine or ten years. The best native
amateur whom I saw during my tour was Mr H.

M. Harriman, and he was very good indeed. But many fine golfers have since arisen in the States, and none better than Mr Jerome Travers, whose style, I thought, was as good as any I had seen in a youthful player.

No doubt the character of golf-course architecture in America has altered a lot since I was there. At that time, it was often primitive and frequently starting in its originality. Asphalt teeing " grounds " were among the features that made me think deeply in the early stages of my visit. They seemed to offer uncomfortably big opportunities for breaking one's favourite driver, and they were responsible for an alteration in my methods, which clung to me for a long while after I returned to England. In order to avoid the danger of hitting the asphalt and so possibly smashing the club, I developed the habit of falling back at the moment of impact. I never tried a low shot against the wind from those teeing " grounds "; the beating down of the ball and consequent contact with the ground just in front of the tee would almost assuredly have meant a detached club-head and a shower of splinters. I always fell back as I made the stroke, thus causing the ball to fly high, and it took me a year or two to thoroughly purge my system of that habit when I settled down again to home golf. Those adamantine starting-places must have been fine things for the club-makers; I should imagine that an inexpert player who could not be sure of hitting the ball cleanly would need to take out about a dozen drivers in order to make sure of having one left intact for the shot to the home hole. But they were by no means good for the golf of a country, and I daresay they have long since ceased to exist.

Strange features of the forest courses were

the teeing grounds built high up in trees. I encountered them on two occasions. They were valuable innovations, since they afforded a sight of the flag where, in the ordinary way, no such guide would have been obtainable. Wonderful creations were some of these courses made in the midst of pine forests. The player had to scale a long flight of steps in order to reach a platform erected in a tree. Then, feeling in this lofty position like a successful Parliamentary candidate who had come out on to the balcony to return thanks to the crowd below, he teed up and drove.

The golfer who makes an extensive tour in the States sees many varieties of the game. Or, at least, his experiences a dozen years ago were amazingly diverse. I believe that great improvements have since been affected and that some of the situations which I found enjoyable by reason of their total unexpectedness no longer present themselves to the seeker of novelty. The Americans have taken heart and soul to the game, and spared neither pains nor money to give to their links an appearance of orthodoxy and a worthy resemblance to British courses. One " green " on which I played consisted of nothing but loose sand from tee to hole, all the way round. It was like a huge hazard, miles long and hundreds of yards wide, it was as though one had committed some awful sin and been sentenced to spend a day in a bunker. No attempt had been made to grow so much as a blade of grass. A heavy roller had been put over the desert, some teeing grounds and holes had been made, and the enthusiasts had gone forth to pursue the game of golf. They were real enthusiasts. That self-same place has now, I understand, a very good course. Some of the

sand putting greens in Florida were far truer than
the great majority that consist of turf. In fact,
they offered no possible excuse for the missing of a putt. A stroke of the right strength
and direction was certain to go down. Baked
by the sun, they were rolled, sprinkled with sand,
and watered twice every day by the hand of
man. The result was the production of a surface as true as that of any billiard table. They
were treated early in the morning and again before the beginning of the afternoon round. Their
thirst was considerable, and the watering was
essential because when they became dry and the
wind started to disturb the sand, they lost all
their beauties. They resolved themselves into
" greens " of grit. Still, when they were good,
they were very good indeed.

It was at St. Augustine, in Florida, that I
first saw land-crabs scuttling about a golf
course. To the man who has grown tired of
condemning worms for their mal-practices, and
allowing grudging approval to sheep and rabbits
for their work as mowers of the fairway, life
takes a new turn when he observes a family party
of crabs ambling around the spot to which he
intends to drive. Still, they are quite reasonable
creatures. At the approach of human footsteps,
they dash off to their holes in the ground. They
lose very little time in the task. They are interesting inhabitants of the links; and it would be a
great relief in this country if, instead of reading
that a ball had been carried off by a crow, we
could learn that it had been seized and taken
underground by a crab. Or that a golfer, instead
of hitting a bird on the wing, had struck a crab
on the claw.

When I was in the States, the turf generally
was not nearly so good as that found in Britain.

It must have considerably retarded the progress of American players. In fact, the standard of their golf twelve years ago was very good considering that they had not long taken up the game in a whole-hearted manner, and that they played under dufficulties as regards the condition of the ground the like of which we seldom experience in this happy land of velvety turf. Improvement in the courses was bound to come; without it, America could hardly have produced such excellent players as she has sent to Britian.

Wherever I went I found evidence of great enthusiasm for the game. Large crowds followed the matches, and I must confess that I was pleasantly surprised by the knowledge which they displayed of the pastime. The people of the States took to golf with boundless zeal and with a fine regard for traditions, and even in those days, I always felt that the onlookers had a real interest in the play and were not merely curious to know what kind of entertainment this golf might be. All the same, they liked something out of the ordinary, and they were keen on an odd, and perhaps purposeless trick, which I was wont to perform for the sake of variety when I was at Ganton. How they came to hear that I had ever done it I do not know; in any case, they liked it. What I used to do was to place a ball lightly at the top of a gorse-bush, so that no branches barred the passage of a club from underneath, take a full swing at it with a driver, and try to hit it straight up into the air so that it would fall within a yard or so of the spot from which it had been despatched. It may have been good training for the eye; it certainly needed a true swing. It may have been rather silly; but anyhow I could send the ball nearly out of sight into the skies, and sometimes make it drop in the same small bush from which I had hit it. Occasionally, too, the scheme very nearly recoiled on my own head—in the literal sense. The Americans heard of the trick, and often insisted upon my doing it. We have all had our youthful absurdities; that was mine.

One point which impressed me in America was the distance that I could drive. I could make the ball "carry" much farther than in this country. The dryer atmosphere of the States offers less resistance to the ball, and if you happen to flatter yourself, when on the other side of the Atlantic, that you have put yards and yards on to your tee-shots, you suffer an awakening when you return home. But these deceptions are constantly inflicted upon the person who travels in pursuit of golf. Thus in the south of France, hazards and holes look farther off—to the eye of the visitor—than they are in point of fact. You take in the situation at a glance, think that you have executed just the right strength of shot, and are disconcerted to see your ball alight on the far side of the green. Still, these things are educational, and are soon learnt.

Golf is going ahead splendidly in Germany, and I have heard the opinion expressed by German players who know the desires of their countrymen, that if some British people who knew all the requirements of course-construction would select a site and lay out a first-glass green near one of the big cities of the Fatherland, the enterprise would be a huge success. So far as my experience goes, the German courses are certainly moderate when judged by our own standard.

In Switzerland, too, the game is making great headway. Montreux, where the golf course is a kind of emerald isle surrounded by snow, may surely be taken as a model by all clubs who find

M

themselves beset with those difficulties which landlords have a way of instituting. In order to secure sufficient ground for twelve extra holes, the Montreux Club had to bargain with eighty-seven landlords. What a time it must have been for the officials. It took three years to successfully complete the negotiations, two of the landowners, whose small plots were situate in the middle of the proposed new course, being possessed with a determination to hold out against even the most tempting offers. Ultimately, however, they gave way, and the committee of the Montreux Club were happy.

Perhaps, sooner or later, I shall go farther afield. From time to time, I have received invitations to visit Australia, South Africa, India and other countries, but they have seemed so very many driver shots away that I have hesitated to leave my native teeing-ground. Golf is now the game of all nations, as it deserves to be. It has no equal, I think, as a test of human strengths and failings. It is not to be mastered by impetuosity. Nor is skill at it to be attained by indifference to its difficulties. I have often seen and heard myself described as a natural golfer. I can only say that in my younger days I practised as assiduously as anybody in the land. Not one of my shots come to me as a gift pure and simple. For two or three years after I became a professional I was always experimenting and thinking out fresh methods of executing strokes —for, in those days, I never saw anybody on whom I could mould my style. Whatever instinct I may have had for golf would never have taken definite shape unless I had pondered a lot and practised a lot. That is the way of the game. There can be no such person in golf as one who plays well without knowing how he does it. A good golfer realizes even to the smallest detail how he obtains his effects. I have set down in this book all that I have learnt in twenty years and more of constant association with the links.   I can only hope that the fruits of my experience will be helpful to many another aspirant to efficiency, and that I shall be able to do just what I have advised—just what I have proved on thousands of occasions to be right—when I play my round on the morrow.

INDEX

ADDRESS: for tee shot, 68
  stooping or crouching
    undesirable, 84
  with mashie, 89
  proper method of ground-
    ing the club, 146, 147
Aim: wrong aim not to be
    confused with pull or
    slice, 154
Amateurs versus Profes-
    sionals, 122 ff
Approach: the most diffi-
    cult part of the game,
    31, 66
  bold approach should be
    encouraged by golf
    architect, 32
  the hole and not the flag
    should be aimed at,
    35
Arms: movement of in
    swing, 72, 73, 77, 83,
    147, 152, 153
  should not be spread too
    far apart, 56
  movement of in mashie
    shot, 91
  in cut mashie shot, 95
  in putting, 103, 106

BADEN-BADEN, 19
Ball: position of in rela-
    tion to feet during
    stroke, 71, 82
  See Gutty, Rubber-cored,
    Haskell, Standardiza-
    tion

Ball, John, 141
Ball, Tom, 104, 106, 163
Boston, 137
Braid, James, 50, 107, 117,
    124, 159-162
Brassie: should be of the
    same lie as driver,
    41; and of the same
    length, 67
  should be stiffer than
    driver, 41
  tends to become too
    whippy after much
    use, 42
  use of on tee, 64, 66
  on fairway, 67
  in cupped lie, 76
Bunker. See Hazard
Byers, E. M., 172

CARRY: should be aimed at
    rather than run, 21 ff,
    26
Clacton-on-Sea, 114
Clay: getting out of, 114
  influence of on methods
    of play, 166
Cleek: should be two or
    three inches shorter
    than driver and
    brassie, 81
  wooden, 85
  value of cleek shot, 78,
    79
  as opposed to iron, 81
Clothes, 49-51

181

Clubs: psychological effect of a new club, 39
choice of, 40, 45
grip of, 48, 49
See Brassie, Driver, etc., Iron Clubs, Wooden Clubs
Course, length of, 32
Cut: with mashie shots, 93-96, 169
in putting, 107

DISTANCE, with iron clubs should be governed by length of back swing, 83, 99
Drainage of golf links, 169, 170
Drive: record drives, length of, 24
preparations for, 46-48
seven golden rules for, 77
should be partly hit as well as swing, 54, 71, 77, 153, 154
with one hand, 151, 152
See Tee shot
Driver: should be of the same lie as brassie, 41; and of the same length, 67
should be whippier than brassie, 41
tends to become too whippy after much use, 41, 42
two drivers should be carried, 42, 43
should not be too long, 44
swing with driver, 43
Driving mashie, as alternative to cleek, 84, 85
Duncan, George, 108, 162

ELBOWS: movement of in swing, 69, 77
for push shot, 127

Evans, C., 172
Eye: keep the eye on the ball, 54, 68

FEET: position of in stance, 147
for slice, 135
for pull, 138
Fingers: place and movement of in swing, 70
Florida, golf in, 175
Follow-through, the, 75
Form, variability of, 39
France, golf in, 172, 177

GANTON, 176
Germany, golf in, 177 ff.
Golf: standard of play deteriorating, 18, 19
popularity of increased by introduction of rubber-cored ball, 17
Grass, long, recovery from, 118, 119
Greens: guarding approach to, 30, 31
back of, 32
flanks of, 33
should be undulating, 36
sand greens in Florida, 175
Grip: on clubs, 48, 49
with hands, importance of good grip, 53, 67, 77
various methods of, 60-62
in swing, 69
in mashie shot, 91
in cut mashie shot, 96
in putting, 105, 106
in pulled shot, 139
faulty grips, 145, 146, 151
Grounding the club, proper method of, 146
Gutty ball, educational value of, 13, 22
See also Rubber-cored ball

HANDS: position of for push shot, 126
  movement of right hand for pulled or sliced shot, 132, 137
  position of for low shot, 140
Harriman, H. M., 172
Haskell ball, introduction of, 16, 17, 24
Hazards: change in occasioned by introduction of rubber-cored ball, 25
  cross hazards, advantages and disadvantages of, 26, 27
  should be placed so as to necessitate carry, 26, 27
  at short holes, 29, 30
  at medium length holes, 31
  at long holes, 31, 32
  diagonal hazards, advantages of, 27, 30
  guarding approach to green—in short holes, 30; in long holes, 30
  guarding back of green, 32
  guarding flanks of green, 33
  should be pleasing to the eye, 34
  pot bunkers, use of, 26, 27, 34
  grass hazards, use of, 35
  bunkers should be deep rather than high, 35
  mounds, use of, 35, 36
  the easiest way out should be played for, 110, 111
  method of play in, 112 ff
  deliberately playing into hazards, occasions for, 116, 117

Hazards—continued.
  playing from mounds, 118
  grass hazards, 118, 119
Head: steadiness of during swing essential, 54-59, 67, 77, 80, 81, 148, 149, 152
  exception to this, 95
Heels: movement of in mashie shot, 88, 91
Herd, Alexander, 16, 84, 109, 162
Herrshoff, F., 172
Hickory, use of for shafts, 45
Hilton, H. H., 122
Hips: movement of in swing, 69, 72, 77, 149, 152
  in mashie shot, 91
  in cut mashie shot, 95
  in sliced shot, 136
Holes: short, number of in model course, 29
  difficulty of, 29, 66
  construction of, 29
  proper length of in model course, 29, 31, 32
Hook. See Pull.
Hoylake, 16, 141

IRON: should be a little shorter than cleek, 81
  iron shots from fairway the easiest in golf, 64, 79
Iron clubs: should be stiff, 44 ff.
  fallacy of using only iron clubs, 44
  grip should be tighter than with wooden clubs, 80
  aim should be taken behind the ball, 83, 92
  stance with, 79, 81 ff.

Iron Clubs—*continued.*
  swing with, 80, 82, 83
  length of shot should be governed by length of swing, 83

KNEES: movement of in mashie shot, 88, 91, 92
  in cut mashie shot, 95

LA BOULIE, 108
Lancewood, use of for shafts, 45
Legs, movement of in stab shot, 118
Lessons, value of, 53
Le Touquet, 172
Low shot, method of procuring, 140

M'EWEN, Peter, 16
Mashie: needs more precision than other clubs, 87
  no more than three-quarter swing desirable, 89, 90
  position of feet during stroke, 90
  method of swing, 91
  should ordinarily be used only when within 100 yards of the hole, 90
  common faults in mashie swing, 92
  use of cut with mashie, 94-96, 169
  running up shot with mashie, 98
  use of on heavy soil, 169
Mashie-niblick, the, 96
Massy, Arnaud, 73, 107, 141, 161
Mid-iron, use of on heavy soil, 168
Mid-Surrey, 35

Montreaux, 177

NEWCASTLE, Co. Down, 142
Niblick: use of in approaching, 96, 97
  in bunkers, 112 ff.
  cut shot with niblick in bunker, 113
  use of by Ray, 158
  use of on heavy soil, 168
Northwood, 97

"OUT OF BOUNDS," precautions against, 48

PARK, Willie, 107
Pitch stroke, change in method of occasioned by introduction of rubber-cored ball, 15, 16, 21
Practice as opposed to match play, value of, 50, 51
Prince's Sandwich, 28
Professionals versus Amateurs, 122 ff.
Pull: intentional, occasions for use of, 131-133
  most people now play for, 42 ff., 139
  teeing for, 48
  dangers of, 133, 134, 138
  method of procuring, 138 ff.
  grip for, 139
  stance for, 138
  unintentional, its cause and cure, 150-152
  should be as severely punished as slice, 33
  not to be confused with faulty aim, 154
Push shot: nature of, 123 ff., 125, 160
  value of, 124 ff., 160

Push shot—*continued.*
can be played with any club, 124, 125
method of accomplishing, 126
no more than three-quarter swing should be attempted, 126
Putter, length of, 108
Putting: concentration of the mind essential to good putting, 36
on an undulating as opposed to a level green, 36
no infallible rules for, 66
the best way to putt, 101, 104
head must be kept still, 101-104
confidence essential, 101, 102
the club should act as a pendulum, 104
the push shot, 105
grip, 105, 106
"Never up, never in," 106
spin, 107
studying the line, 107
a cure for bad putting, 101, 102, 107
amateurs versus professionals, 109
Putting green. *See* Green.

QUILL, Colonel, 57. 68 149

RADCLIFFE-ON-TRENT, 164
Ray, Edward, 157 ff.
"Road" hole, the, at St Andrews, 116
Robson, Fred, 163
Rough, a greater embarrassment than bunkers. 33

Rubber-cored ball, effect of introduction of, 14 ff., 36, 52
amount of extra length obtained by, 24
See Haskell.
Run. *See* Carry
Running up, method of, 98

ST ANDREWS, 34, 109, 116
Sand, getting out of, 112 ff.
Sandwich, 106
Schlaffing, its cause and cure, 153
Seaside as opposed to inland links, 130, 131
Shafts: 48, 49
of lancewood, 45
of hickory, 45
Sherlock, James, 162, 163
Shoulders: movement of in swing, 74, 77
in mashie shot, 92
in sliced shot, 135
Slice, intentional: to be preferred to pull, 134, 135
teeing for, 48
occasions for use of, 131-133
method of procuring, 135-137
stance for, 135
unintentional: punishment of, 33
must not be confused with faulty aim, 154
its cause and cure, 149, 150
Socketing: remedy for, 153
South Herts, 169
Spoon: as alternative to cleek, 84, 85
use of on heavy soil, 168
Stab shot, the, 118
Stance: change in occasioned by introduc-

Stance—*continued*.
   tion of rubber-cored ball, 20 ff.
   with wooden clubs depends on lie of club, 41
   choice of on teeing ground, 46
   for tee shot, 68, 69
   for mashie shot, 89, 90
   for cut mashie shot, 94
   for getting out of bunkers, 112
   for push shot, 126 ff.
   for sliced shot, 135
   for pulled shot, 138
   for low shot, 140
   for high shot, 140
   common faults in, 146 ff.
Standardization of ball, 14-16
Stoke Poges, 162
Style : change in occasioned by introduction of rubber-cored ball, 14 ff., 20 ff., 25
Swing : changes in occasioned by introduction of rubber-cored ball, 17, 20, 22
   with driver, 43
   steadiness of head during swing essential, 54-59, 68, 77, 80, 81, 148, 149, 152
   should contain an element of hitting, 54, 71, 77, 153, 154
   an art, 64
   varieties of, 64, 65
   St Andrews swing, the, 64
   " flat " swing, the, 65
   the first thing to be learnt in golf, 66
   proper method of, 68 ff., 75
   upward swing, the, 69-72, 75.

Swing—*continued*.
   downward swing, the, 72· 74
   common faults, 74
   follow-through, the, 75
   length of, should govern distance in iron shots, 83, 84
   stooping or crouching undesirable, 84
   for mashie shot, 91
   for getting out of bunkers, 111, 112
   for push shot, 126 ff.
   for sliced shot, 136
Switzerland : golf in, 177

TAYLOR, J. H., 50, 107, 114, 142, 161 ff.
Tee : making of, 46, 47
   place of on teeing-ground, 48
   for high shot, 140
   for low shot, 140
   asphalt teeing grounds, 173
   in trees, 174
Tee shot : at short holes, 29
   choice of stance for, 46, 47
   method of making identical with that of shot on fairway, 66
Topping : its cause and cure, 148, 149
Totteridge, 169
Travers, J. D., 172, 173
Travis, W. J., 106, 172

UNITED STATES : golf in 172 ff.

VARDON, Tom, 163

WALTON HEATH, 124
White, Jack, 107
Williamson, Tom, 164

Wooden clubs, lie of, 41
  grip should be looser than
    with iron clubs, 80
Wrists: movement of in
    swing, 72, 77, 150,
    151

Wrists—*continued*.
  in mashie shot, 92, 93
  in cut mashie shot, 96
  in putting, 104, 106
  in push shot, 127

Printed by
MORRISON & GIBB LIMITED
Edinburgh

Printed in the United States
151912LV00003B/140/A

9 781432 590192